Hymns

FROM

THE LAND OF LUTHER.

Translated from the German.

NEW AND ENLARGED EDITION.

New-York:
A. D. F. RANDOLPH & CO.,
770 BROADWAY.
1869.

A FEW of the following poems may be considered as rather *imitations* than translations, although the ideas and structure are too much borrowed to allow them to be called original. It is hoped this small Selection may give pleasure to some who are not acquainted with the German language, and lead others to explore farther for themselves its treasures of devotional poetry

EDINBURGH, December, 1853.

CONTENTS.

From Page 113.

Hymns from the Land of Luther.

JOYS TO COME.

"Wird das nicht Freude seyn!"

"Everlasting joy shall be upon their heads: they shall obtain gladness and joy."—Isa. 51 : 11.

Will that not joyful be,
When we walk by faith no more,
When the Lord we loved before,
As Brother-man we see;
When He welcomes us above,
When we share His smile of love,
Will that not joyful be?

Will not that joyful be,
When to meet us rise and come,
All our buried treasures home,
A gladsome company!
When our arms embrace again,
Those we mourned so long in vain,
Will that not joyful be?

Will that not joyful be,
When the foes we dread to meet,
Every one beneath our feet
We tread triumphantly!
When we never more can know
Slightest touch of pain or woe,
Will that not joyful be?

Will that not joyful be,
When we hear what none can tell,
And the ringing chorus swell
Of angels' melody!
When we join their songs of praise,
Hallelujahs with them raise,
Will that not joyful be?

Yes! that will joyful be;
Let the world her gifts recall,
There is bitterness in all:
Her joys are vanity!
Courage, dear ones of my heart!
Though it grieves us here to part,
There we will joyful be!

H. C. von Schweinitz.

DYING PETITIONS.

"Gedenke mein, mein Gott."

"Remember me, my God! remember me,
In hour of deepest woe;
Thou art my only hope, my only plea,
Against th' accusing foe.
Oh! show me now Thy full salvation,
Oh! hear my dying supplication!
Remember me!"

"I think on thee, believer! tremble not,
Thy Saviour still is near:
Here is my cross, my blood to cleanse each spot,
My promises to cheer.
Is not my love unchanged, unshaken?
How shall mine own be e'er forsaken?
I think on thee!"

"Remember me! man's help can naught avail
In the dark valley's shade;
My strength must faint, my flesh and heart must fail,
Oh! haste Thou to mine aid!
Silence and darkness o'er me stealing,
Oh! be Thou still thyself revealing,—
Remember me!"

"I think on thee! soon in the better land
Thou shalt with me rejoice;
The harps of heaven are waiting for thy hand,
The chorus for thy voice:
The angel bands are round thee bending,
Thy parting spirit close attending,—
I think on thee!"

"Remember me! by Thine own hour of pain,
Appear in mine to save
Smooth for my rest the couch where Thou hast lain,
The pillow of the grave;
And while the years of time are flying,
In that lone place of darkness lying,—
Remember me!"

"I think on thee! thine own Redeemer lives,
Thy hope shall not be vain:
When the last trump its solemn summons gives,
Thou shalt arise again.
Now, go in peace, securely sleeping,
Thy dust is safe in angels' keeping,—
I think on thee!"

"Remember me, and the afflicted band
Whom I must leave behind!
Pour consolation from Thine own rich hand
On mourning heart and mind.
Oh! hear this one, this last petition,
Then shall I go in glad submission,—
Remember me."

I think on thee! with that sad band of love
I will in mercy deal;
My tender sympathy their souls shall prove
My Spirit's power to heal.
The long-sought bliss shall yet be given,
The lost of earth are found in heaven,—
I think on thee!"

"Now, sweetly sleep! angels thy soul receive,
And bear to Jesus' breast!
Long in our hearts thy memory shall live,
Here let thy body rest.
Secure from earthly pain and sorrow,
Till dawns the resurrection morrow.
Now, sweetly sleep!"

UNBEKANNTES.

WEEP NOT.

"Weine nicht!"

"The Lord hath heard the voice of my weeping."—Psalm 6 : 8.

Weep not—Jesus lives on high,
O sad and wearied one!
If thou with the burden sigh,
Of grief thou canst not shun,
Trust Him still,
Soon there will
Roses in the thicket stand,
Goshen smile in Egypt's land.

Weep not—Jesus thinks of thee
When all beside forget,
And on thee so lovingly
His faithfulness has set,
That though all
Ruin'd fall,
Every thing on earth be shaken,
Thou wilt never be forsaken.

Weep not—Jesus heareth thee,
Hears thy moanings broken,
Hears when thou right wearily
All thy grief hast spoken.
Raise thy cry,
He is nigh,

And when waves roll full in view,
He shall fix their "Hitherto."

Weep not—Jesus loveth thee,
  Though all around may scorn,
And though poison'd arrows be
  Upon thy buckler borne,
          With His love,
          Naught can move;
All may fail—yet only wait,
He shall make the crooked straight.

Weep not—Jesus cares for thee,
  Then what of good can fail?
Why shouldst thou thus gloomily
  At thought of trouble quail?
          He will bear
          All thy care;
And if He the burden take,
He will all things perfect make.

Weep not—Jesus comforts thee,
  He yet shall come and save,
And each sorrow thou shalt see
  Lie buried in thy grave.
          Sin shall die,
          Grief shall fly,
Thou hast wept thy latest tears
When the Lord of life appears!

B. Schmolk

HERE IS MY HEART!

"HIER ist mein Herz."

"MY son, give me thine heart."—PROV. 23 : 26.

HERE is my heart!—my God, I give it Thee;
I heard Thee call and say,
'Not to the world, my child, but unto me,"—
I heard, and will obey.
Here is love's offering to my King,
Which in glad sacrifice I bring.
Here is my heart.

Here is my heart!—surely the gift, though poor,
My God will not despise;
Vainly and long I sought to make it pure,
To meet Thy searching eyes:
Corrupted first in Adam's fall,
The stains of sin pollute it all.
My guilty heart!

Here is my heart!—my heart so hard before,
Now by Thy grace made meet;
Yet bruised and wearied, it can only pour
Its anguish at Thy feet;

It groans beneath the weight of sin,
It sighs salvation's joy to win.
My mourning heart!

Here is my heart!—in Christ its longings end,
Near to His cross it draws;
It says, "Thou art my portion, O my friend!
Thy blood my ransom was."
And in the Saviour it has found
What blessedness and peace abound.
My trusting heart!

Here is my heart!—ah! Holy Spirit, come,
Its nature to renew,
And consecrate it wholly as Thy home,
A temple fair and true.
Teach it to love and serve Thee more,
To fear Thee, trust Thee, and adore.
My cleansed heart!

Here is my heart!—it trembles to draw near
The glory of Thy throne;
Give it the shining robe Thy servants wear,
Of righteousness Thine own:
Its pride and folly chase away,
And all its vanity, I pray.
My humbled heart!

Here is my heart!—teach it, O Lord, to
cling
In gladness unto Thee;
And in the day of sorrow still to sing,
"Welcome, my God's decree."
Believing, all its journey through,
That Thou art wise, and just, and true.
My waiting heart!

Here is my heart!—O Friend of friends,
be near
To make each tempter fly;
And when my latest foe I wait with fear,
Give me the victory!
Gladly on Thy love reposing,
Let me say, when life is closing,
"Here is my heart!"

EHRENFRIED LIEBICH.

DISCIPLINE.

"ZAGE nicht."

TREMBLE not, though darkly gather
Clouds and tempests o'er thy sky,
Still believe thy Heavenly Father
Loves thee best when storms are nigh

When the sun of fortune shineth
Long and brightly on the heart,
Soon its fruitfulness declineth,
Parched and dry in every part.

Then the plants of grace have faded
In the dry and burning soil;
Thorns and briers their growth have shaded—
Earthly cares and earthly toil.

But the clouds are seen ascending;
Soon the heavens are overcast;
And the weary heart is bending
'Neath affliction's stormy blast.

Yet the Lord, on high presiding,
Rules the storm with powerful hand;
He the shower of grace is guiding,
To the dry and barren land.

See, at length the clouds are breaking—
Tempests have not pass'd in vain;
For the soul, revived, awaking,
Bears its fruits and flowers again.

Love divine nas seen and counted
Every tear it caus'd to fall,
And the storm which love appointed,
Was its choicest gift of all.

A MOTHER'S PRAYER IN THE NIGHT.

Darkness reigns—the hum of life's commotion
On the listening ear no longer breaks;
Stars are shining on the deep blue ocean,
All is silent—Love alone awakes.

Love on earth its lonely vigils keeping,
Love in heaven, that rests or slumbers not;
Peace, my anxious heart! though thou wert sleeping,
Love divine has ne'er its charge forgot.

And for you, my brightest earthly flowers,
You, my children, Love divine has cared;
Sleep, beloved ones! through these dark hours—
Angels by your pillow watch and guard.

Here the winged messengers of heaven,
As beheld at Bethel, come and go—
Angel guardians, whom the Lord has given,
To each little one while here below.

Thou, O Saviour, while on earth residing,
Never didst Thou scorn a mother's prayer:

Faith may still behold Thee here abiding—
  Still commend her treasures to Thy care.

Were not all my hope on Thee reposing,
  Thou sole refuge for a sinner's fears,
Then, the future all its ill disclosing,
  I could give my children only tears.

From their earthly parents they inherit
  Naught save sin and weakness, grief and pain:
Give them, Lord, thine all-sufficient merit,
  Spiritual birth and life again.

Hide and guard them in Thy tender arms,
  Till the wilderness of life be past;
Save them from temptation's fatal charms,
  Seal them for Thine own, from first to last.
Let Thy rod and staff in mercy lead them
  In the footsteps of Thy flock below,
Till 'mid heavenly pastures Thou shalt feed them,
  Where the streams of life eternal flow.

CHRISTOPHE AGTE.

JESUS, STILL LEAD ON.

"Jesu, geh voran."

"They forsook all, and followed him."—Luke 5 : 11.

Jesus, still lead on,
Till our rest be won!
And although the way be cheerless,
We will follow, calm and fearless.
Guide us by thy hand
To our Fatherland.

If the way be drear,
If the foe be near,
Let not faithless fears o'ertake us,
Let not faith and hope forsake us:
For, through many a foe,
To our home we go!

When we seek relief
From a long-felt grief—
When oppressed by new temptations,
Lord, increase and perfect patience.
Show us that bright shore
Where we weep no more!

Jesus, still lead on,
Till our rest be won!

Heavenly Leader, still direct us,
Still support, console, protect us,
Till we safely stand
In our Fatherland!

LUDWIG VON ZINZENDORF.

TO A DYING CHILD.

"ZEUCH-HIN, mein Kind."

DEPART, my child! the Lord thy spirit calls
To leave a world of woe:
Sad on my heart the heavenly summons falls,
Yet since He wills it so,
I calm the rising agitation,
And say, with humble resignation,
Depart, my child!

Depart, my child! lent for a little while
Our drooping hearts to cheer;
Dear is thy loving voice, thy gentle smile,
Ah! who can tell how dear?
The sands are run, too quickly falling:
The Giver comes, His own recalling.
Depart, my child!

Depart, my child! enjoy in heaven's pure
day
What earth must still deny;
Here many a storm awaits thy longer
way,
And many a tear thine eye.
Go, where the flowers have never faded,
Where love may smile unchilled, unshaded.
Depart, my child!

Depart, my child! soon shall we meet
again
In the good land of rest:
Thou goest, happy one! ere grief or pain
Have reached thy gentle breast.
Happy, our thorny path forsaking,
From life's vain dream so early waking.
Depart, my child!

Depart, my child! angels are bending
down
To set thy spirit free;
The Saviour holds in heaven the golden
crown
He won on earth for thee.
Yes! now in Him thou art victorious:
Go, share His rest and triumph glorious.
Depart, my child!

GOTTFRIED HOFFMANN.

ARISE!

"Wachet auf."

ARISE! ye lingering saints, arise!
  Remember that the might of grace,
When guilty slumbers sealed your eyes,
  Awakened you to run the race;
And let not darkness round you fall,
But hearken to the Saviour's call.
Arise!

Arise! because the night of sin
  Must flee before the light of day;
God's glorious Gospel, shining in,
  Must chase the midnight gloom away:
You can not true disciples be
If you still walk in vanity.
Arise!

Arise! although the flesh be weak,
  The spirit willing is and true,
And servants of the Master seek
  To follow where it guideth to.
Beloved! oh, be wise indeed,
And let the spirit ever lead.
Arise.

Arise! because our Serpent-foe,
  Unwearied, strives by day and night,

Remembers time is short below,
  And wrestles on with hellish might.
Then boldly grasp both sword and shield:
Who slumbers on the battle-field?
Arise!

Arise! before that hour unknown—
  The hour of death that comes ere long,
And comes not to the weak alone,
  But to the mighty and the strong.
Beloved! oft in spirit dwell
Upon the hour that none can tell.
Arise!

Arise! that you prepared may stand,
  Before the coming of the Lord;
The day of wrath draws nigh at hand,
  According to th' eternal Word.
Ah! think, perhaps this day shall see
The dawning of eternity!
Arise!

Arise! it is the Master's will:
  No more His heavenly voice despise,
Why linger with the dying still?
  He calls—Arouse you, and arise!
No longer slight the Saviour's call,
It sounds to you, to me, to all.
Arise!

LUDWIG GOTTER.

GOD WITH ME.

"GOTT bei mir in jedem Ort."

"WHEN thou passest through the waters, I will be with thee; and through the rivers, they shall not overflow thee; when thou walkest through the fire, thou shalt not be burned; neither shall the flame kindle upon thee."—ISA. 43 : 2.

MY God with me in every place!
 Firmly does the promise stand,
On land or sea, with present grace
 Still to aid us near at hand.
 If you ask, "Who is with thee?"
 God is here—my God with me!

No depth, nor prison, nor the grave,
 Can exclude Him from His own;
His cheering presence still I have,
 If in crowds or all alone.
 In whatever state I be,
 Everywhere is God with me!

My God for me! I dare to say—
 God the portion of my soul!
Nor need I tremble in dismay
 When around me troubles roll.
 If you ask, "What comforts thee?"
 It is this—God is for me!

Ah! faith has seen Him cradled lie,
 Here on earth a weeping child;

Has seen Him for my vileness die—
He, the sinless, undefiled!
And thus I know it true to be,
God, my Saviour, is for me!

In life, in death, with God so near,
Every battle I shall win,
Shall boldly press through dangers here,
Triumph over every sin!
"What!" you say, "a victor be?"
No, not I, but God in me!

C. F. ZELLER.

THE COMMUNION OF SAINTS.

"BLESSED are the dead which die in the Lord from henceforth: Yea, saith the Spirit, that they may rest from their labors; and their works do follow them."—REV. 14 : 13.

"O WIE selig seyd ihr doch, ihr Frommen."

CHURCH ON EARTH.

"OH! how blessed are ye, saints forgiven,
Through the gate o death now safe in heaven,
All trials over,
All the ills, which round us darkly hover!"

CHURCH IN HEAVEN.

"Yes, dear friends, our joys are still increasing,
Our songs of praise are new and never ceasing,
All preparing
For the time when you shall all be sharing."

CHURCH ON EARTH.

"We are now as in a prison dwelling,
Storms of care and trouble o'er us swelling;
All around us
Only sins and griefs, to snare and wound us."

CHURCH IN HEAVEN.

"Ah, beloved friends! be not complaining,
Wish not joy while still on earth remaining,
Be still confiding
In your Father's love and tender guiding."

CHURCH ON EARTH.

"In your quiet home so gently resting,
Safe for evermore from all molesting,

No care or sorrow
Can *you* feel to-day, or fear to-morrow!"

CHURCH IN HEAVEN.

"In your conflicts we were once engaging,
Long with sin and Satan warfare waging;
All your distresses
Once were ours, to weary and oppress us."

CHURCH ON EARTH.

"Christ has wiped away your every tear;
You enjoy what we are seeking here,
The harps of heaven
Sound in strains to mortals never given."

CHURCH IN HEAVEN.

"Yet in patience run the race before you,
Long for heaven, where Love is watching o'er you:
Sow in weeping—
Soon the fruit with joy you shall be reaping."

CHURCH ON EARTH.

"Come, come quickly, long expected Jesus,
From all sin and sorrow to release us,

Quickly take us
To Thyself, and blest for ever make us!"

CHURCH IN HEAVEN.

"Ah, beloved souls! your palms victorious,
Golden harps, and thrones of triumph glorious,
All are waiting:
Follow on with courage unabating."

CHORUS.

"Let us join to praise His name for ever,
To us both of every good the Giver.
Life undying
We shall each obtain, on Him relying.

"Praise Him, men on earth, and saints in heaven!
To the Lamb be praise and glory given—
Praise unending,
Glory through eternity extending!"

SIMON DACH.

EVENING HYMN.

"Nun ruhen alle Waelder."

QUIETLY rest the woods and dales,
Silence round the hearth prevails,
The world is all asleep:
Thou, my soul, in thought arise,
Seek thy Father in the skies,
And holy vigils with Him keep.

Sun, where hidest thou thy light?
Art thou driven hence by Night,
Thy dark and ancient foe?
Go! another Sun is mine—
Jesus comes with light divine,
To cheer my pilgrimage below.

Now that day has passed away,
Golden stars in bright array
Bespangle the blue sky:
Bright and clear, so would I stand,
When I hear my Lord's command
To leave this earth, and upward fly.

Now this body seeks for rest,
From its vestments all undrest,
Types of mortality:
Christ shall give me soon to wear,
Garments beautiful and fair—
White robes of glorious majesty.

Head, and feet, and hands, once more
Joy to think of labor o'er,
And night with gladness see.
O my heart! thou too shalt know
Rest from all thy toil below,
And from earth's turmoil soon be free.

Weary limbs, now rest ye here;
Safe from danger and from fear,
Seek slumber on this bed:
Deeper rest ere long to share,
Other hands shall soon prepare
My narrow couch among the dead.

While my eyes I gently close,
Stealing o'er me soft repose,
Who shall my guardian be?
Soul and body now I leave,
(And Thou wilt the trust receive,)
O Israel's Watchman! unto Thee.

O my friends! from you this day
May all ill have fled away,
No danger near have come.
Now, my God, these dear ones keep;
Give to my beloved sleep,
And angels send to guard their home!

PAUL GERHARD.

MY GOD! I KNOW THAT I MUST DIE.

"Mein Gott! ich weiss wohl dass ich sterbe."

Job 14: 11, 12.

My God! I know that I must die—
My mortal life is passing hence
On earth I neither hope nor try
To find a lasting residence.
Then teach me by Thy heavenly grace,
With joy and peace my death to face.

My God! I know not *when* I die,
What is the moment or the hour—
How soon the clay may broken lie,
How quickly pass away the flower;
Then may Thy child prepared be
Through time to meet Eternity.

My God! I know not *how* I die,
For death has many ways to come—
In dark mysterious agony,
Or gently as a sleep to some.
Just as Thou wilt! if but it be
For ever blessed, Lord, with Thee.

My God! I know not *where* I die,
Where is my grave, beneath what strand,
Yet from its gloom I do rely
To be delivered by Thy hand.
Content, I take what spot is mine,
Since all the earth, my Lord, is Thine.

My gracious God! when I must die,
Oh! bear my happy soul above,
With Christ, my Lord, eternally
To share Thy glory and Thy love!
Then comes it right and well to me,
When, where, and how my death shall be.

B. SCHMOLK.

LIGHT IN DARKNESS.

"ALL things work together for good to them that love God."—ROM. 8 : 28.

How weary and how worthless this life at times appears!
What days of heavy musings, what hours of bitter tears!
How dark the storm-clouds gather along the wintry skies!
How desolate and cheerless the path before us lies!

And yet these days of dreariness are sent
us from above:
They do not come in anger, but in faithfulness and love;
They come to teach us lessons which bright
ones could not yield,
And to leave us blest and thankful when
their purpose is fulfilled.

They come to draw us nearer to our Father
and our Lord,
More earnestly to seek His face, to listen
to His word.
And to feel, if now around us a desert land
we see,
Without the star of promise, what would
its darkness be!

They come to lay us lowly, and humbled in
the dust,
All self-deception swept away, all creature-
hope and trust;
Our helplessness, our vileness, our guilti-
ness to own,
And flee, for hope and refuge, to Christ, and
Christ alone.

They come to break the fetters which here
detain us fast,
And force our long reluctant hearts to rise
to heaven at last·

And brighten every prospect of that eternal
home,
Where grief and disappointment and fear
can never come.

Then turn not in despondence, poor weary
heart, away,
But meekly journey onwards, through the
dark and cloudy day;
Even now the bow of promise is above
thee painted bright,
And soon a joyful morning shall dissipate
the night.

Thy God hath not forgot thee, and, when
He sees it best,
Will lead thee into sunshine, will give thee
bowers of rest;
And all thy pain and sorrow, when the
pilgrimage is o'er,
Shall end in heavenly blessedness, and joys
for evermore! SPITTA.

LET ME FIND THEE!

"SEEK ye the Lord while he may be found."—ISA. 55:6

"SIEH, hier bin ich, Ehren-Koenig."

BEHOLD me here, in grief draw near,
 Pleading at Thy throne, O King!
To Thee each tear, each trembling fear,
 Jesus, Son of man! I bring.
Let me find Thee,—let me find Thee—
 Me, a vile and worthless thing!

Look down in love, and from above,
 With Thy Spirit satisfy;
Thou hast sought me, Thou hast bought me
 And Thy purchase, Lord, am I.
Let me find Thee,—let me find Thee,
 Here on earth, and then on high!

No other prayer to Thee I bear,
 O my Lord, but only this:
To share Thy grace, to see Thy face,
 And to know Thy people's bliss.
Let me find Thee,—let me find Thee—
 Thee to find is blessedness!

Hear the broken, scarcely spoken
 Utterance of my heart to Thee;
All the crying, all the sighing,
 Of Thy child accepted be.

Let me find Thee,—let me find Thee:
  Thus my soul longs vehemently!

Worldly pleasures, earthly treasures,
  Joys and honors, will not stay;
They often pain, and, oh! how vain,
  Looking to eternity!
Let me find Thee,—let me find Thee,
  Find Thee, O my God, this day!

JOACHIM NEANDER.

GRIEF AND CONSOLATION BY A MOTHER'S DEATH-BED.

"KLAGE und Trost."

"NEVER couldst thou bear to grieve us—
  Dearest mother, why to-day?
Wherefore wilt thou thus forsake us,
  Why, oh! why refuse to stay?"
  "Were it but our Father's will,
  Gladly had I tarried still."

"Mother, see the bursting anguish
  Of thy dear ones, loved so well;
See our eyes with grief o'erflowing—
  Grief which words refuse to tell!"
  "Children, bid me not remain:
  Let me see our Carl again!"

"Ah! and art thou really going
To that dark and distant shore?
All *our* cares, our joys, our sorrows,
All forgotten, shared no more!"
"Children, think not, say not so—
To the land of *love* I go."

"From the circle of affection,
Mother, must thou next depart?
Ah! how many a link is broken
Once uniting heart to heart!"
"Closer draw that gentle chain
Round the lov'd who yet remain."

'Canst thou then so gladly leave us?
Is our grief unheeded now?
For thine eye is brightly beaming,
Calm and cloudless is thy brow."
"Yes! for faith, and hope, and love,
Draw me to my Lord above."

Yet even there, in bliss undying,
When thou numberest thine own,
Mother, shall not *we* be wanting—
We, who here in bondage groan?"
"Come, beloved! quickly come,
Join me in our heavenly home!"

Möwes

AH! GRIEVE NOT SO.

"GODLINESS with contentment is great gain."—1 TIM. 6

"NICHT so traurig, nicht so sehr."

AH! grieve not so, nor so lament,
My soul! nor troubled sigh,
Because some joys to others sent
Thy Father may deny;
Take all as love that seems severe—
There is no want if God is near.

There is no right thou canst demand,
No title thou canst claim;
For all are strangers in the land
Who bear the human name:
Earth and its treasures are the Lord's,
And He the lot of each accords.

How thankless art thou, child of man!
For favors that abound;
Thy God has given thee eyes to scan
The glory all around;
Yet seldom for this priceless sight,
Hast thou been heard to praise aright.

Number thy limbs, thy members tell,
And ask thy thankless soul,
If to another thou wouldst sell
The smallest of the whole.

There is not one from which thy heart
Would willingly submit to part.

Now, go and search the depths of mind,
Explore its wondrous power,
New proofs of benefits to find,
That meet thee every hour;
More than the sand upon the shore,
And ever rising more and more.

He knows, who lives on Zion's hill,
What we in truth require;
Knows too how many blessings still
This flesh and blood desire;
And could He safely all bestow,
He would not let thee sorrowing go.

Thou wert not born that earth should be
A portion fondly sought;
Look up to heaven, and smiling see
Thy shining, golden lot!
Honors and joys, which thou shalt share,
Unending and unenvied there!

Then journey on to life and bliss,
God will protect to heaven;
And every good that meets thee is
A blessing wisely given.
If losses come, so let it be—
The God of heaven remains with thee.

PAUL GERHARD

PILGRIM SONG.

"Here we have no continuing city, but seek one to come."
—Heb. 13 : 14.

"Kommt, Kinder, lasst uns gehen."

Come, brothers, let us onward—
Night comes without delay;
And in this howling desert
It is not good to stay.
Take courage, and be strong,
We are hasting on to heaven:
Strength for warfare will be given,
And glory won ere long.

The Pilgrim's path of trial
We do not fear to view;
We know His voice who calls us,
We know Him to be true.
Then, let who will contemn,
But, strong in His almighty grace,
Come, every one, with steadfast face,
On to Jerusalem!

If we would walk as pilgrims,
We must not riches heap—
Much treasure to have gathered
But makes the way more steep.

We march with laggard speed
Till every weight is cast aside—
Till with the little satisfied
That pilgrimage can need.

Here, all unknown we wander,
Despised on every hand,
Unnoticed, save when slighted
As strangers in the land.
Our joys they will not share,
Yet sing,—that they may catch the song
Of heaven, and the happy throng
That now await us there!

Come, gladly let us onward,
Hand in hand still go,
Each helping one another
Through all the way below.
One family of love,
Oh! let no voice of strife be heard,
No discord, by the angel-guard
Who watch us from above.

O brothers! soon is ended
The journey we've begun;
Endure a little longer,
The race will soon be run.
And in the land of rest,
In yonder bright, eternal home,
Where all the Father's loved ones come,
We shall be safe and blest!

Then boldly let us venture—
This, this is worth the cost,
Though dangers we encounter,
Though every thing is lost.
O world! how vain thy call!
We follow Him who went before—
We follow, to th' eternal shore,
Jesus, our All in All!

GERHARD TERSTEEGEN.

MY FATHER IS THE MIGHTY LORD.

"ALL things are yours."—1 COR. 3 : 21.

"MEIN Vater ist der grosse Herr der Welt."

MY Father is the mighty Lord, whose arm
Spans earth and sky, and shields His child from harm—
Whose still, small voice of love is yet the same
As once from Horeb's fiery mount it came—
Whose glorious works the angel-choirs declare.
He hears their praise, and hearkens to my prayer.

My King is God's eternal, holy Son,
And He anoints me as a chosen one;
He has redeemed me with His precious blood,
And for unnumber'd debts has surety stood;
He fought the foe, and drew me by His hand,
Out from his camp, into His Father's land.

My brotherhood's a circle, stretching wide
Around one fount, although a sea divide;
With fathers, who behold the Lord in light,
With saints unborn, who shall adore His might,
With brothers, who the race of faith now run,
In union and communion, I am one!

My journey's end lies upward and afar;
It glimmers bright, but vaguely as a star;
And oft as faith has caught some glimpse serene,
So often clouds and mists obscure the scene;
Yet, in this longing ends each vision dim—
To see my Lord, and to be made like Him!

My grave, so long a dark and drear abyss,
Is now scarce noticed on the way to bliss;

Once at the gates of Hell it yawning lay,
Now stands as portal to the land of day;
It takes me to the Father's home so blest;
It brings me to the feast, a welcome guest.

LANGE.

THY WILL BE DONE.

"It is the Lord; let him do what seemeth him good."
—1 Sam. 3:18.

"Mein Jesu, wie du willt!"

My Jesus, as Thou wilt!
  Oh! may Thy will be mine!
Into Thy hand of love
  I would my all resign.
Through sorrow, or through joy,
  Conduct me as Thine own,
And help me still to say,
  My Lord, Thy will be done!

My Jesus, as Thou wilt!
  If needy here and poor,
Give me Thy people's bread,
  Their portion rich and sure.
The manna of Thy word
  Let my soul feed upon,
And if all else should fail—
My Lord, Thy will be done!

My Jesus, as Thou wilt!
  If among thorns I go,
Still sometimes here and there
  Let a few roses blow.
But Thou on earth along
  The thorny path hast gone,
Then lead me after Thee.
  My Lord, Thy will be done!

My Jesus, as Thou wilt!
  Though seen through many a tear,
Let not my star of hope
  Grow dim or disappear.
Since Thou on earth hast wept
  And sorrowed oft alone,
If I must weep with Thee,
  My Lord, Thy will be done!

My Jesus, as Thou wilt!
  If loved ones must depart,
Suffer not sorrow's flood
  To overwhelm my heart:
For they are blest with Thee,
  Their race and conflict won:
Let me but follow them.
  My Lord, Thy will be done!

My Jesus, as Thou wilt!
  When death itself draws nigh,
To thy dear wounded side
  I would for refuge fly.

Leaning on Thee, to go
  Where Thou before hast gone;
The rest as Thou shalt please.
  My Lord, Thy will be done!

My Jesus, as Thou wilt!
  All shall be well for me:
Each changing future scene
  I gladly trust with Thee.
Straight to my home above
  I travel calmly on,
And sing, in life or death,
  My Lord, Thy will be done!

BENJAMIN SCHMOLK.

THE GOOD SHEPHERD.

"I WILL feed my flock, and I will cause them to lie down, saith the Lord God."—EZEK. 34:15.

"JA fuerwahr! uns fuehrt mit sanften Hand
Ein Hirt durch Pilger-land."

YES! our Shepherd leads with gentle hand,
  Through the dark pilgrim-land,
  His flock, so dearly bought,
  So long and fondly sought.
      Hallelujah!

When in clouds and mist the weak ones
stray,
He shows again the way,
And points to them afar
A bright and guiding star.
Hallelujah!

Tenderly He watches from on high
With an unwearied eye;
He comforts and sustains,
In all their fears and pains.
Hallelujah!

Through the parch'd, dreary desert He will
guide
To the green fountain-side;
Through the dark, stormy night,
To a calm land of light.
Hallelujah!

Yes! His "little flock" are ne'er forgot;
His mercy changes not:
Our home is safe above,
Within His arms of love.
Hallelujah!

KRUMMACHER.

REJOICE.

"BEHOLD, the Bridegroom cometh; go ye out to meet Him."—MATT. 25 : 6.

"ERMUNTERT euch, ihr Frommen."

REJOICE, all ye believers,
And let your lights appear;
The evening is advancing,
And darker night is near.
The Bridegroom is arising,
And soon He draweth nigh.
Up! pray, and watch, and wrestle—
At midnight comes the cry!

See that your lamps are burning,
Replenish them with oil,
And wait for your salvation,
The end of earthly toil.
The watchers on the mountain
Proclaim the Bridegroom near;
Go, meet Him as He cometh,
With Hallelujahs clear!

Ye wise and holy virgins,
Now raise your voices higher,
Till in songs of jubilee
They meet the angel-choir.

The marriage-feast is waiting,
The gates wide open stand;
Up! up! ye heirs of glory—
The Bridegroom is at hand!

Ye saints, who here in patience
Your cross and suff'rings bore,
Shall live and reign for ever,
When sorrow is no more.
Around the throne of glory,
The Lamb ye shall behold,
In triumph cast before Him
Your diadems of gold!

Palms of victory are there;
There, radiant garments are;
There stands the peaceful harvest,
Beyond the reach of war.
There, after stormy winter,
The flowers of earth arise,
And from the grave's long slumber
Shall meet again our eyes!

Our Hope and Expectation,
O Jesus! now appear;
Arise, thou Sun, so longed for,
O'er this benighted sphere!
With hearts and hands uplifted,
We plead, O Lord, to see
The day of earth's redemption,
That brings us unto thee!

LAURENTIUS LAURENTI

THE ANGEL AND THE INFANT.

SMILING, a bright-eyed seraph bent
  Over an infant's dream;
To view his mirrored form he leant
  As in the crystal stream.

"Fair infant, come," he whispered low,
  "And leave the earth with me;
To a bright and happy land we'll go—
  This is no home for thee.

"Each sparkling pleasure knows alloy,
  Nor cloudless skies are here;
A care there is for every joy,
  For every smile a tear.

"The heart that dances free and light,
  May soon be chained by sorrow;
The sun that sets in calm to-night,
  May rise in storm to-morrow.

"Alas! to cloud a brow so fair,
  That griefs and pains should rise!
Alas! that this dark world of care
  Should dim these laughing eyes!

"To seek a brighter land with me,
Infant, thou wilt not fear;
For piteous Heaven the sad decree
Recalls, that sent thee here."

It seemed on him the sweet babe smiled·
His wings the seraph spread:
They're gone—the angel and the child.
Poor mother! thy son is dead!

UNBEKANNTER.

THE SERVICE OF THE LORD.

"DER Dienst der Herrn."

"IF any man serve me, let him follow me; and where I am, there shall also my servant be."—JOHN 12 : 26.

How blessed, from the bonds of sin
And earthly fetters free,
In singleness of heart and aim,
Thy servant, Lord, to be!
The hardest toil to undertake
With joy at Thy command!
The meanest office to receive
With meekness at Thy hand!

With willing heart and longing eyes,
  To watch before Thy gate,
Ready to run the weary race,
  To bear the heavy weight;
No voice of thunder to expect,
  But follow calm and still,
For love can easily divine
  The One Beloved's will.

Thus may I serve Thee, gracious Lord
  Thus ever Thine alone,
My soul and body given to Thee,
  The purchase Thou hast won:
Through evil or through good report
  Still keeping by Thy side,
By life or death, in this poor flesh
  Let Christ be magnified!

How happily the working days
  In this dear service fly!
How rapidly the closing hour,
  The time of rest, draws nigh!
When all the faithful gather home,
  A joyful company,
And ever where the Master is,
  Shall His blest servants be.

SPITTA

THE DESIRED HAVEN.

"LORD, now lettest Thou Thy servant depart in peace, according to Thy word."—LUKE 2 : 29.

"Lord, the waves are breaking o'er me and around;
Oft of coming tempests I hear the moaning sound:
Here there is no safety, rocks on either hand;
'Tis a foreign roadstead, a strange and hostile land.
Wherefore should I linger? others, gone before,
Long since safe are landed on a calm and friendly shore:
Now the sailing orders in mercy, Lord, bestow—
Loose the cable, let me go!

"Lord, the night is closing round my feeble bark;
How shall I encounter its watches long and dark?
Sorely worn and shattered by many a billow past,
Can I stand another rude and stormy blast?

Ah! the promised haven I never may attain,
Sinking and forgotten amid the lonely main;
Enemies around me, gloomy depths below.
Loose the cable, let me go

"Lord, I would be near Thee, with Thee where Thou art—
Thine own word hath said it, 'tis 'better to depart,'
There to serve Thee better, there to love Thee more,
With thy ransomed people to worship and adore.
Ever to Thy presence Thou dost call Thine own—
Why am I remaining, helpless and alone?
Oh! to see Thy glory, Thy wondrous love to know!
Loose the cable, let me go!

"Lord, the lights are gleaming from the distant shore,
Where no billows threaten, where no tempests roar.

Long beloved voices calling me I hear—
Oh! how sweet *their* summons falls upon
  my ear!
Here are foes and strangers, faithless
  hearts and cold,
There is fond affection, fondly proved of
  old!
Let me haste to join them: may it not
  be so?
  Loose the cable, let me go!"

Hark, the solemn answer! hark, the pro-
  mise sure!
"Blessed are the servants who to the
  end endure!
Yet a little longer hope and tarry on—
Yet a little longer, weak and weary one!
More to perfect patience, to grow in faith
  and love,
More *my* strength and wisdom, and faith-
  fulness to prove:
Then the sailing orders the Captain *shall*
  bestow—
  Loose the cable, let thee go!"

UNBEKANNTES.

THE LONG GOOD-NIGHT.

"HAVING a desire to depart, and to be with Christ; which is far better."—PHIL. 1 : 23.

"ICH fahr dahin mit Freuden."

I JOURNEY forth rejoicing,
From this dark vale of tears,
To heavenly joy and freedom,
From earthly bonds and fears:
Where Christ our Lord shall gather
All His redeemed again,
His kingdom to inherit.
Good-night, till then!

Go to thy quiet resting,
Poor tenement of clay!
From all thy pain and weakness
I gladly haste away;
But still in faith confiding
To find thee yet again,
All glorious and immortal.
Good-night, till then!

Why thus so sadly weeping,
Belov'd ones of my heart?
The Lord is good and gracious,
Though now He bids us part.

Oft have we met in gladness,
And we shall meet again,
All sorrow left behind us
Good-night, till then!

I go to see His glory,
Whom we have loved below;
I go, the blessed angels,
The holy saints to know.
Our lovely ones departed,
I go to find again,
And wait for you to join us.
Good-night, till then!

I hear the Saviour calling—
The joyful hour has come,
The angel-guards are ready
To guide me to our home,
Where Christ our Lord shall gather
All His redeemed again,
His kingdom to inherit.
Good-night, till then!

UNBEKANNTER

ALL THINGS ARE YOURS.

"For all things are yours; whether Paul, or Apollos, or Cephas, or the world, or life, or death, or things present, or things to come; all are yours."—1 Cor. 3 : 21, 22.

"Alles ist euer!—O Worte des ewigen Lebens."

All things are yours! Oh! sweet message
of mercy divine!
Christian brothers, rejoice in your portion
and mine!
Ours the high prize,
Which poor sinners despise,
And for a vain world resign.

Raise your affections and heart to your
home in the sky,
Then let the earth and its vanities wither
and die;
Your joys shall last,
When theirs are long past—
Your treasure is laid up on high.

All things are yours, my beloved! our Lord
from above
Watches his people with tender compassion
and love.
Hear his dear voice:
"My brethren, rejoice!
Nothing your safety shall move!'

All of things present that earth and her
fulness can yield,
All of things future from knowledge and
fancy concealed,
Life's varied tale,
Death's dark, dreaded vale,
All as your portion revealed!

Heaven and earth, and the sea, and the
systems of light,
Spirits unnumbered, angelic hosts holy and
bright,
All are for thee,
Brother! be joyful with me,
Let us in praises unite!

Does thy heart sink in the conflict with fear
and despair?
Are tears overflowing from fountains of
sorrow and care?
On yonder shore,
See, they are weeping no more—
Old things have passed away there!

Praise to the Saviour, whose death our sal-
vation secures!
Praise to the Father, whose mercy for ever
endures!
New songs of praise
Evermore let us raise.
Amen! yes, all things are yours!

SCHUBART.

THE WIDOW OF NAIN.

"AND when the Lord saw her, he had compassion on her, and said unto her, Weep not."—LUKE 7 : 13.

"O SUSSES Wort."

OH! sweetest words that Jesus could have sought,
To soothe the mourning widow's heart, "Weep not!"
They fall with comfort on my ear,
When life is dark and trouble near.

They were not whispered accents, but aloud
The Saviour spake them to the silent crowd,
That each might hear His heavenly voice,
And in the widow's joy rejoice!

Words, that were spoken amid sorrow's strife,
And in the very midst of death and life;
They shall refresh my soul at last,
And strengthen me till life is past.

If poverty obscures my earthly lot,
Then shall I hear my Saviour say, "Weep not."

To God the Father raise thine eye,
For still He hears the raven's cry.

And, oh! should persecution's ruthless hand
Grant me no quiet possession in the land,
The voice of Jesus calms each thought—
Heaven is thy dwelling-place: "Weep not!"

Though death the dearest of my heart hath slain,
Jesus shall yet restore my dead again;
"Weep not," He says, "poor weary one,
But think what I at Nain have done!"

When I myself am drawing near to death,
This Jesus shall be there, and thus He saith:
"The race is run, the battle fought,
I am thy light, thy life: 'Weep not!'"

Oh! sweetest words that Jesus could have sought,
To cheer His weary troubled ones· "Weep not!"
Thrice blessed words! I listening stay,
Till grief and sorrow flee away!

DR. JOHANN HOFEL

CONFLICT.

"WHY art thou cast down, O my soul? and why art thou disquieted within me? hope thou in God; for I shall yet praise Him, who is the health of my countenance, and my God."—PSALM 43 : 5.

"SCHOENE Sonne, kommst du endlich wieder?"

SUN of comfort, art thou fled for ever?
  Light of joy, wilt thou return at last?
Shall I sing again the song of morning,
  When the watches of the night are past?
Ah! delay not, long-expected dawning!
  Scatter the thick clouds and mist away,
Which so dark on feeling and devotion,
  Over heart and memory rest to-day!

Weeping I have stood alone in darkness,
  Gloomy cliffs above, and depths below
On the narrow pathway all forsaken,
  Left to wrestle with the accusing Foe.
Doubt and unbelief, and dark forebodings,
  Fearful spectres gathering around;
Ah! my dizzy brain and foot were failing,
  Tottering over the abyss profound!

Yet One held me back! An arm almighty,
  Strong to save, as Satan to destroy!
From the giddy precipice He caught me,
  Drew me from despair to life and joy.

Jesus was my Helper! Saving mercy
  Is His work, His glory, His delight;
Many a chain of darkness He has broken,
  Changed to sunshine many a dismal night.

I will trust *again* His love, His power,
  Though I can not *feel* His hand to-day;
To His help anew I will betake me,
  Though His countenance seem turned away!
Though without one smile, one gracious token,
  Through the flames and floods my path must go;
When the fires subside, the waves pass over,
  My Deliverer I again shall know.

Yes, the light of comfort shall return,
  Joy's sweet sun shall shine again at last;
I shall sing the gladsome song of morning,
  When the watches of the night are past;
It shall reäppear, the welcome dawning,
  Scattering the clouds and mist away,
Which so dark on feeling and devotion,
  Over heart and memory rest to-day!

I shall find again the hopes long vanished,
  Like the swallows when the storms are gone

Fountains shall be opened in the desert,
Streams by the wayside, while journeying on.
Flowers of love and promise shall be springing
Where the cruel thorn and wormwood sprung,
And the *homeward path* lie bright in sunshine,
Where my sad harp on the willows hung.

LANGE.

LOVE TO CHRIST.

"WHOM having not seen ye love."—1 PET. 1 : 8.

"ICH will Dich lieben."

I WILL love Thee, all my treasure!
I will love Thee, all my strength!
I will love Thee without measure,
And will love Thee right at length.
Oh! I will love Thee, Light Divine,
Till I die and find Thee mine!

Alas! that I so lately knew Thee—
Thee, so worthy of the best;
Nor had sooner turned to view Thee,
Truest Good, and only Rest!

The more I love, I mourn the more
That I did not love before!

Far I ran, and wander'd blindly,
Seeking some created light;
Then I sought, but I could not find Thee—
I had wandered from Thee quite;
Until at last Thou art made known
Through Thy seeking, not my own!

I will praise Thee, Sun of Glory!
For Thy beams have gladness brought.
I will praise Thee, will adore Thee,
For the light I vainly sought;
Will praise Thee that Thy words so blest
Spake my sin-sick soul to rest!

In Thy footsteps now uphold me,
That I stumble not nor stray.
When the narrow way is told me,
Never let me ling'ring stay.
But come my weary soul to cheer,
Shine, Eternal Sunbeam, here!

Be my heart more warmly glowing,
Sweet and calm the tears I shed;
And its love, its ardor showing,
Let my spirit onward tread.
Still near to Thee, and nearer still,
Draw this heart, this mind, this will.

I will love, in joy and sorrow!
  Crowning joy! will love Thee well,
I will love to-day, to-morrow,
  While I in this body dwell!
Oh! I will love Thee, Light Divine,
Till I die and find Thee mine!

JOHANN ANGELUS.

PARTING.

"WHAT mean ye to weep, and to break mine heart?"—ACTS 21 : 13.

"WAS macht ihr, dass ihr weinet."

WHAT mean ye by this wailing,
  To break my bleeding heart?
As if the love that binds us
  Could alter or depart!
Our sweet and holy union
  Knows neither time nor place;
The love that God has planted
  Is lasting as His grace.

Ye clasp these hands at parting,
  As if no hope could be;
While still we stand for ever
  In blessed unity!

Ye gaze, as on a vision
  Ye never could recall,
While still each thought is with you,
  And Jesus with us all!

Ye say, "We here, thou yonder,
  Thou goest, and we stay!"
And yet Christ's mystic body
  Is one eternally.
Ye speak of different journeys,
  A long and sad adieu!
While still one way I travel,
  And have one end with you!

Why should ye now be weeping
  These agonizing tears?
Behold our gracious Leader,
  And cast away your fears.
We tread *one* path to glory,
  Are guided by *one* hand,
And led in faith and patience
  Unto *one* Fatherland!

Then let this hour of parting
  No bitter grief record,
But be an hour of union
  More blessed with our Lord!
With Him to guide and save us,
  No changes that await,
No earthly separations
  Can leave us desolate!

SPITTA.

THE ANGEL OF PATIENCE.

"Ye have need of patience.—Heb. 10 : 36."

"Es zieht ein stiller Engel durch dieses Erdenland."

A gentle Angel walketh throughout world of woe,
With messages of mercy to mourning hearts below;
His peaceful smile invites them to love and to confide,
Oh! follow in His footsteps, keep closely by His side!

So gently will He lead thee through all the cloudy day,
And whisper of glad tidings to cheer the pilgrim-way;
His courage never failing, when thine is almost gone,
He takes thy heavy burden, and helps to bear it on.

To soft and tearful sadness He changes dumb despair,
And soothes to deep submission the storm of grief and care;

Where midnight shades are brooding He
pours the light of noon,
And every grievous wound He heals, most
surely, if not soon.

He will not blame thy sorrows, while He
brings the healing balm;
He does not chide thy longings, while He
soothes them into calm;
And when thy heart is murmuring, and
wildly asking why?
He smiling beckons *forward*, points upward to the sky.

He will not always answer thy questions
and thy fear,
His watchword is "Be patient, the journey's end is near!"
And ever through the toilsome way, He
tells of joys to come,
And points the pilgrim to his rest, the
wanderer to his home. SPITTA.

LOOKING HOME.

"Having a desire to depart."—Phil. 1 : 23.

"Ach, uns wird das Herz so leer."

Ah! this heart is void and chill
  'Mid earth's noisy thronging—
For the Father's mansions still
  Veh'mently is longing!

In the garments once so strong,
  Now are rents distressing;
And the sandals borne so long,
  Heavily are pressing.

Oh! to be at home, and gain
  All for which we're sighing—
From all earthly want and pain
  To be swiftly flying.

With this load of sin and care,
  Then no longer bending,
But with waiting angels there,
  On our Lord attending!

Ah! how blessed, blessed they
  Who have rightly striven,
And rejoice eternally
  With their Lord in heaven!

Spitta.

MORNING HYMN.

"My voice shalt thou hear in the morning, O Lord."—Psalm 5 : 3.

"Morgen glanz der Ewigkeit."

Jesus, Sun of righteousness,
  Brightest beam of Love Divine,
With the early morning rays
  Do Thou on our darkness shine,
And dispel with purest light
All our night!

As on drooping herb and flower
  Falls the soft refreshing dew,
Let Thy Spirit's grace and power
  All our weary souls renew;
Showers of blessing over all
Softly fall!

Like the sun's reviving ray,
  May Thy love, with tender glow,
All our coldness melt away,
  Warm and cheer us forth to go,
Gladly serve Thee and obey
All the day!

O our only Hope and Guide!
  Never leave us nor forsake:

Keep us ever at Thy side,
  Till the eternal morning break,
Moving on to Zion hill
Homeward still!

Lead us all our days and years
  In Thy straight and narrow way;
Lead us through the vale of tears
  To the land of perfect day,
Where Thy people, fully blest,
Safely rest! KNOV. VON RO[illegible]OTH.

RECALL.

"RETURN, ye backsliding children, and I will h[illegible] [illegible] backslidings."—JER. 3 : 22.

"KEHRE wieder, kehre wieder."

RETURN, return!
Poor, long lost wanderer, home!
  With all thy bitter tears,
Thy heavy burdens, come!
As thou art all sin and pain,
Fear not to implore in vain:
See, the Father comes to meet thee,
  Points to mercy's open door;
Words of life and promise greet thee
Ah! return, delay no more!

Return, return!
From strife and tumult vain
To quiet solitude,
To silent thought again.
There the storms shall sink to rest
Which now desolate thy breast;
There the Spirit, long neglected,
Waits with bliss before unknown;
And the Saviour, long rejected,
Claims and seals thee for His own.

Return, return!
From all thy crooked ways;
Jesus will save the lost,
The fallen He can raise.
Look to Him, who beckons thee
From the cross so lovingly.
See His gracious arms extended;
Fear not to seek shelter there,
Where no grief is unbefriended,
Where no sinner need despair.

Return, return!
To thy long-suffering Lord.
Fear not to seek His grace,
To trust His faithful word;
Yield to Him thy weary heart—
He can heal its keenest smart;
He can soothe the deepest sorrow
Wash the blackest guilt away:
Then delay not till to-morrow,
Seek His offered gifts to-day.

Return, return!
From all thy wanderings, home!
From vanity and toil,
To rest and substance, come!
Come to Truth from Error's night,
Come from darkness unto light,
Come from death to life undying,
From a fallen earth to Heaven—
Now the accepted time is flying,
Haste to take what God has given!

SPITTA.

GOING HOME.

"But I would not have you to be ignorant, brethren, concerning them which are asleep, that ye sorrow not, even as others which have no hope."—1 Thess. 4:13.

"Unser Lieben sind geschieden."

Our beloved have departed,
While we tarry broken-hearted,
In the dreary, empty house;
They have ended life's brief story,
They have reached the home of glory,
Over death victorious!

Hush that sobbing, weep more lightly,
On we travel, daily, nightly,
To the rest that they have found.

Are we not upon the river,
Sailing fast to meet for ever,
On more holy, happy ground?

Whilst with bitter tears we're mourning,
Thought to buried loves returning,
Time is hasting us along,
Downward to the grave's dark dwelling,
Upward to the fountain welling
With eternal life and song!

See ye not the breezes hieing?
Clouds along in hurry flying?
But *we* haste more swiftly on—
Ever changing our position,
Ever tossed in strange transition—
Here to-day, to-morrow gone!

Every hour that passes o'er us
Speaks of comfort yet before us,
Of our journey's rapid rate;
And like passing vesper-bells,
The clock of time its chiming tells,
At eternity's broad gate.

On we haste, to home invited,
There with friends to be united
In a surer bond than here;
Meeting soon, and met for ever!
Glorious hope! forsake us never,
For thy glimmering light is dear

Ah! the way is shining clearer
As we journey ever nearer
To the everlasting home.
Friends, who there await our landing,
Comrades, round the throne now stand-
ing,
We salute you, and we come!

LANGE

THE JOURNEY TO JERUSALEM.

"AND they were in the way going up to Jerusalem; and Jesus went before them; and they were amazed; and as they followed, they were afraid."—MARK 10:32.

"JESU, was hat dich getrieben."

JESUS! what was that which drew Thee
To Jerusalem's ancient gate?
Ah! the love that burned so truly,
Would not suffer Thee to wait!
On Thou journeyedst, thus securing
Me a city more enduring!

To my spirit now draw nearer,
Lord, as to Jerusalem!
Let each moment prove Thee dearer;
Make this heart a Bethlehem!
Thus my Saviour's love, possessing,
Surely I have Salem's blessing!

To the world Thou hast sent me,
  Like the twelve that saw Thy face
Lead me through the journey gently,
  Keep me near Thee by Thy grace.
My allotted work fulfilling,
Ever ready, ever willing.

Let me gladly see my calling,
  When and where Thou sendest me,
Never into darkness falling,
  Gazing on futurity;
But obey when Thou hast bidden,
Though Thy counsel should be hidden.

Let me follow Thee, my Saviour,
  Not with words or empty show;
But my heart, my life, behavior,
  Prove Thy presence here below.
Meekly with the froward bearing,
And each brother's burden sharing!

Oh, my Lord! if Thou shouldst ever
  Call me desolate to roam,
For Thy truth and conscience sever
  Every tie of house and home,
Then draw nearer, if Thou smite me;
Let not crosses disunite me.

So shall I, hosannahs singing,
  All the desert-way rejoice

Late and early, praises bringing,
But with feeble, earthly voice.
Though these broken notes distress me,
Jesus! Thou wilt hear and bless me!

LAURENTIUS LAURENTI.

THE MERCHANT.

"AGAIN, the kingdom of heaven is like unto a merchantman seeking goodly pearls: who, when he had found one pearl of great price, went and sold all that he had, and bought it."—MATT. 13 : 45, 46.

"EINEN Kaufmann sieht man ohne Gleichen."

ONCE a merchant travelled far and wide,
Over mountain-chains and ocean's tide;
Slighted and despised on every hand,
Wearily he passed from land to land.

Not with treasure treasures to acquire,
Seemed the wanderer's purpose or desire;
Gold and silver he regarded not—
Pearls alone with eagerness he sought.

Many were produced to meet his call;
Strictly he examined, weighed them all;
Nothing could deceive, or please his eye:
Calmly he surveyed, and passed them by.

Sadly he pursued his search around—
Ah! the *One* midst many was not found!
Stars indeed he saw, but not the Sun
All his longings sought and dwelt upon.

Weary now with all his wanderings vain,
To his native home he turns again;
There he finds a Fisher on the strand,
Stooping down to draw a net to land.

What new treasures of the deep are these?
Who this unknown Stranger of the seas?
Changed His aspect now, His bearing high,
While He speaks with gentle dignity:

"Peace be with thee! Now thou mayest
obtain
All so long desired and sought in vain—
Thou 'mid many fools the only wise,
At thy journey's end behold the prize!"

"Yes, it is the One, beyond compare,
Sought so long, abandoned in despair;
Stranger, speak, how may it be my own?'
"*All thou hast* can be the price alone."

"Be it so!" he joyfully replied;
"Lord, take all, and take myself beside!
For in wondrous love Thou bring'st from
heaven
What no monarch has or could have given."

And the world deceived and foolish call
Him, who for one jewel gave his all;
But unheeding what they think or say,
Glad and satisfied he goes his way.

Food is his which they have never known—
Cordials granted to himself alone:
From earth's vanities and cares set free,
Now he walks in peace and liberty.

Wondrous blessings reach him from above;
Love comes down to meet the heart of love;
Ever as he views his treasure bright,
All his soul is filled with life and light.

Blessed they who find the priceless gem!
Blessed they who seek! It shines for them
Brightly still, the prize by God revealed,
For the victor on Faith's battle-field.

FROM THE KIRCHEN-FREUNDE.

SUBMISSION.

"In your patience possess ye your souls."—Luke 21 : 19.

"Stille, mein Wille! dein Jesu hilft siegen."

Be still, my soul!—the Lord is on thy side;
Bear patiently the cross of grief and pain;
Leave to thy God to order and provide—
In every change He faithful will remain.
Be still, my soul!—thy best, thy Heavenly Friend
Through thorny ways leads to a joyful end.

Be still, my soul!—thy God doth undertake
To guide the future, as He has the past:
Thy hope, thy confidence, let nothing shake,
All now mysterious shall be bright at last.
Be still, my soul!—the waves and winds still know
His voice who ruled them while He dwelt below.

Be still, my soul!—when dearest friends depart,
And all is darkened in the vale of tears,

Then shalt thou better know His love, His heart,
  Who comes to soothe thy sorrow and thy fears.
Be still, my soul!—thy Jesus can repay
From His own fulness all He takes away.

Be still, my soul!—the hour is hastening on
  When we shall be for ever with the Lord—
When disappointment, grief, and fear are gone,
  Sorrow forgot, Love's purest joys restored.
Be still, my soul!—when change and tears are past,
All safe and blessed we shall meet at last.

Be still, my soul!—begin the song of praise
  On earth, believing, to thy Lord on high;
Acknowledge Him in all thy works and ways,
  So shall He view thee with a well-pleased eye.
Be still, my soul!—the Sun of life divine
Through passing clouds shall but more brightly shine.

UNBEKANNTES.

THE BELIEVER'S DYING TESTAMENT.

"I AM now ready to be offered, and the time of my departure is at hand."—2 TIM. 4 : 6.

"ICH habe Lust zu scheiden."

WEARY, waiting to depart,
  My spirit longs for flight;
Still I gaze with throbbing heart
  To Zion's fields of light.
When His summons shall be sent,
  No dweller here may know—
To my dying testament,
  Friends, hearken, ere I go!

God, my Father, to Thy hand
  This spirit I bequeath;
Guide it through this desert land,
  And through the gates of death.
By Thy gift this soul was mine—
  Take it to Thyself again,
So shall it for ever Thine
  In life and death remain.

What, O Jesus, shall I make
  An offering to Thee?
Ah! these sins, these sorrows take,
  So grievous, Lord, to me.

In the crimson stream that flows,
  My Saviour, from Thy side,
Thus my faith each burden throws,
  Hide them, for ever, hide!

O thou Spirit of all might!
  I yield Thee my last sigh,
And to Thee, in death's dread fight,
  I send my latest cry!
As life's pulses steal away,
  Oh! speak peace to me!
And let my fainting soul that day
  Nothing save Jesus see.

Angels, take these flowing tears
  From my pale cheeks away!
Ye can pity earth-born fears,
  And gladly will obey.
Bear me to my Saviour's care,
  In these kind arms of love,
And let me for ever share
  Your tearless bliss above.

Ye beloved ones, and true,
  Who weeping round me bend,
Though I go, I leave with you
  Your everlasting Friend.
Take my parting blessing, then,
  And weep for me no more—
Surely we shall meet again
  On the eternal shore!

Earth, poor earth, I've spent on thee
  A long and clouded day:
Take as my last legacy,
  This dwelling-house of clay;
In thy keeping it must fall
  To humble dust once more,
But, ere long, thy graves shall all
  In living truth restore!

This is my last testament—
  God! fix Thy seal thereto!
Now I wait in calm content,
  With heaven full in view.
Resting on my Lord in faith,
  I pass securely on,
Knowing when I conquer death
  My heritage is won!

B. SCHMOLK.

WAITING.

"MINE hour is not yet come."—JOHN 2. 4

"MEINE stund ist noch nicht kommen."

"JESUS' hour is not yet come;"
  Let this word thine answer be,
Pilgrim, asking for thy home,
  Longing to be blest and free.
Yet a season tarry on—
Nobly borne is nobly done.

While oppressing cares and fears,
  Night and day no respite leave,
Still prolonged through many years,
  None to help thee or relieve,
Hold the word of promise fast,
Till deliverance comes at last.

Every creature-hope and trust,
  Every earthly prop or stay,
May lie prostrate in the dust,
  May have failed or passed away;
Then when darkness falls the night,
Jesus comes, and all is light.

Yes, the Comforter draws nigh
  To the breaking, bursting heart,
For, with tender sympathy,
  He has seen and felt its smart:
Through its darkest hours of ill,
He is waiting, watching still.

Dost thou ask, *When* comes His hour?
  Then, when it shall aid thee best.
Trust His faithfulness and power,
  Trust in Him and quietly rest.
Suffer on, and hope, and wait—
  Jesus never comes too late.

Blessed day, which hastens fast,
  End of conflict and of sin

Death itself shall die at last,
  Heaven's eternal joys begin.
Then eternity shall prove,
God is Light, and God is Love. SPITTA.

PRAISE AND PRAYER.

"If any man be in Christ, he is a new creature; old things are passed away; behold all things are become new."—2 Cor. 5:17.

"O treuer Heiland Jesu Christ."

We praise and bless Thee, gracious Lord,
  Our Saviour kind and true,
For all the old things passed away,
  For all Thou hast made new.

The old security is gone,
  In which so long we lay;
The sleep of death Thou hast dispelled,
  The darkness rolled away.

New hopes, new purposes, desires,
  And joys, Thy grace has given;
Old ties are broken from the earth,
  New ones attach to heaven.

But yet how much must be destroyed,
  How much renewed must be,
Ere we can fully stand complete
  In likeness, Lord, to Thee!

Ere to Jerusalem above,
  The holy place, we come,
Where nothing sinful or defiled
  Shall ever find a home!

Thou, only Thou, must carry on
  The work Thou hast begun:
Of Thine own strength Thou must impart,
  In Thine own ways to run.

Ah! leave us not—from day to day
  Revive, restore again;
Our feeble steps do Thou direct,
  Our enemies restrain.

Whate'er would tempt the soul to stray,
  Or separate from Thee,
That, Lord, remove, however dear
  To the poor heart it be!

When the flesh sinks, then strengthen Thou
  The spirit from above;
Make us to feel Thy service sweet,
  And light Thy yoke of love.

So shall we faultlesss stand at last
Before Thy Father's throne,
The blessedness for ever ours,
The glory all Thine own!

SPITTA.

CALVARY.

"SURELY he hath borne our griefs, and carried our sorrows."
—ISAIAH 53 : 4.

"FLIESST, ihr Augen, Fliesst von Thranen."

FLOW, my tears, flow still faster,
Thus my guilt and sin bemoan;
Mourn, my heart, in deeper anguish,
Over sorrows not thine own!
See, a spotless Lamb draw nigh
To Jerusalem to die;
For thy sins, the sinless One;
Think! ah! think what thou hast done!

See Him stand while cruel fetters
Bind the hands that framed the world,
While around Him bitter mocking,
Laughter and contempt are hurled.
Heathen rage and Jewish scorn,
Meekly for our sins are borne.
Sin has brought Him from above:
Who can fathom such a love?

Soon the heavy doom is spoken,
Even Pilate's pleading ceased,
Jesus to the cross is chosen,
And Barabbas is released!
Ah! there is no loving word,
Not one voice of pity heard!
But the loud and frenzied cry,
"Crucify Him, crucify!"

Can we view the Saviour given
To the smiter's hands for us?
Can we all unmoved, unhumbled,
See Him mocked and slighted thus?
View the thorny chaplet made,
For His meek and silent head,
Hear the loud and angry din,
And not tremble for our sin?

Follow from the hall of judgment
This sad Saviour on His way;
But, in spirit, as ye journey,
Often pause, and humbly pray;
Pray the Father to behold
By the Son thy ransom told,
And a Substitute for thee,
In His Well-beloved see!

Must I, Jesus, thus behold Thee
In Thy toil and sorrow here?
Can I nothing better yield Thee
Than my unavailing tear?

Lamb of God! I weep for Thee!
Weep, Thy cruel cross to see!
Weep, for death that death destroys!
Weep, for grief that brings me joys!

Poor is all that I can offer—
Soul and body while I live;
Take it, O my Saviour, take it—
I have nothing more to give.
Come, and in this heart remain;
Let each enemy be slain;
Let me live and die with Thee;
To Thy kingdom welcome me.

Loud and louder saints are singing,
Glory! glory! Christ, to Thee!
Over death and hell for ever
Thou hast triumphed gloriously.
I am Thine, and Thou art mine:
Oh! to see Thy brightness shine!
Lord! Thy day of grief is o'er,
Come in glory—come once more!

LAURENTIUS LAURENTI.

REÜNION.

"I SHALL go to him."—2 SAM. 12 : 23.

"WIEDERSEHN! ja, wiedersehn wird einst."

MEET again! yes, we shall meet again,
Though now we part in pain!
His people all
Together Christ shall call.
Hallelujah!

Soon the days of absence shall be o'er,
And thou shalt weep no more;
Our meeting day
Shall wipe all tears away.
Hallelujah!

Now I go with gladness to our home,
With gladness thou shalt come;
There I will wait
To meet thee at heaven's gate.
Hallelujah!

Dearest! what delight again to share
Our sweet communion there!
To walk among
The holy ransomed throng.
Hallelujah!

Here, in many a grief, our hearts were one,
But there in joys alone;
    Joy fading never,
    Increasing, deepening ever.
        Hallelujah!

Not to mortal sight can it be given
To know the bliss of heaven;
    But thou shalt be
    Soon there, and sing with me,
        Hallelujah!

Meet again! yes, we shall meet again,
Though now we part in pain!
    Together all
    His people Christ shall call.
        Hallelujah!

M. A. ZILLE

JESUS ALL-SUFFICIENT.

"THE Lord is my portion, saith my soul."—LAM. 3 : 24.

"WENN ich Ihn nur habe."

    If only He is mine—
      If but this poor heart
    Never more, in grief or joy,
      May from Him depart,
Then farewell to sadness,
All I feel is love, and hope, and gladness.

If only He is mine,
Then from all below,
Leaning on my pilgrim-staff,
Gladly forth I go
From the crowd who follow
In the broad, bright road, their pleasures false and hollow.

If only He is mine,
Then all else is given;
Every blessing lifts my eyes
And my heart to heaven.
Fill'd with heavenly love,
Earthly hopes and fears no longer tempt to move.

There, where He is mine,
Is my Fatherland,
And my heritage of bliss
Daily cometh from His hand.
Now I find again
In His people love long lost, and mourn'd in vain.

NOVALIS

ANTICIPATION.

"Beloved, now are we the sons of God: and it doth not yet appear what we shall be."—1 John 3 : 2.

"Wie wird mir seyn?"

What shall I be, my Lord, when I behold
Thee
In awful majesty at God's right hand,
And 'mid th' eternal glories that enfold
me,
In strange bewilderment, O Lord, I
stand?
What shall I be?—these tears, they dim my
sight,
I can not catch the blissful vision right.

What shall I be, Lord, when Thy radiant
glory,
As from the grave I rise, encircles me;
When brightly pictured in the light before
me,
What eye hath never seen, my eyes shall
see?
What shall I be? Ah! blessed and sub
lime
Is the dim prospect of that glorious time!

What shall I be, when days of grief are
ended,
From earthly fetters set for ever free;
When from the harps of saints and angels
blended,
I hear the burst of joyful melody?
What shall I be, when, risen from the
dead,
Sin, death, and hell I never more shall
dread?

What shall I be, when all around are
thronging
The loved of earth, where I have come
to dwell;
When all is joy and praise—no anxious
longing,
No bitter parting, and no sad farewell?
What shall I be? Ah! how the streaming
light
Can lend a brightness to this dreary night!

Yes; faith can never know the full salva-
tion,
Which Jesus for His people will prepare;
Then will I wait in peaceful expectation,
Till the Good Shepherd comes to take
me there.
My Lord, my God, a blissful end I see,
Though now I know not what I yet shall
be! LANGBECKER.

GOD CALLING YET.

"Unto you, O men, I call; and my voice is to the sons of man."—Prov. 8 : 4.

"Gott rufet noch!"

God calling yet! — and shall I never
hearken,
But still earth's witcheries my spirit
darken?
This passing life, these passing joys, all
flying,
And still my soul in dreamy slumbers
lying!

God calling yet!—and I not yet arising,
So long His loving, faithful voice despising;
So falsely His unwearied care repaying:
He calls me still, and still I am delaying.

God calling yet! — loud at my door is
knocking,
And I my heart, my ear, still firmer lock-
ing:
He still is ready, willing to receive me,
Is waiting now, but ah! He soon may
leave me.

God calling yet!—and I no answer giving;
I dread His yoke, and am in bondage living;
Too long I linger, but not yet forsaken,
He calls me still. O my poor heart, awaken!

Ah! yield Him all—all to His care confiding:
Where but with Him are rest and peace abiding?
Unloose, unloose, break earthly bonds asunder,
And let this spirit rise in soaring wonder.

God calling yet! I can no longer tarry,
Nor to my God a heart divided carry;
Now, vain and giddy world, your spells are broken—
Sweeter than all, the voice of God has spoken!

GERHARD TERSTEEGEN.

RESIGNATION.

"WHAT! shall we receive good at the hand of God, and shall we not receive evil?"—JOB 2 : 10.

"ICH hab' in guten Stunden."

I HAVE had my days of blessing,
All the joys of life possessing,
Unnumber'd they appear!
Then let faith and patience cheer me,
Now that trials gather near me:
Where is life without a tear?

Yes, O Lord, a sinner looking
O'er the sins Thou art rebuking,
Must own Thy judgments light.
Surely I, so oft offending,
Must, in humble patience bending,
Feel Thy chastisements are right.

Let me, o'er transgression weeping,
Find the grace my soul is seeking;
Receiving at Thy throne
Strength to meet each tribulation,
Looking for the great salvation,
Trusting in my Lord alone!

While 'mid earthly tears and sighing,
Still to praise Thee feebly trying,
Still clinging, Lord, to Thee:

Quietly on Thy love relying,
I am Thine—and, living, dying,
Surely all is well with me!

CHRISTIAN FURCHTEGOTT GELLERT.

REST.

"WE which have believed do enter into rest."—HEB. 4 : 3.

"ICH bleib bei Dir! wo koennt ich 's besser haben!"

I REST with Thee, Lord! whither should I go?
I feel so blest within Thy home of love!
The blessings purchased by Thy pain and woe,
To Thy poor child Thou sendest from above.
Oh! never let Thy grace depart from me:
So shall I still abide, my Lord, with Thee.

I rest with Thee! Eternal life the prize
Thou wilt bestow, when faith's good fight is won;
What can earth give but vain regrets and sighs,
To the poor heart whose passing bliss is done?

For lasting joys I fleeting ones resign,
Since Jesus calls me His, and He is mine.

I rest with Thee! No other place of rest
Can now attract, no other portion please.
The soul, of heavenly treasure once possest,
All earthly glory with indifference sees.
Poor world, farewell! thy splendors tempt no more—
The power of grace I feel, and thine is o'er,

I rest with Thee! with Thee, whose wondrous love
Descends to seek the lost, the fallen raise,
Oh! that my whole of future life might prove
One hallelujah, one glad song of praise!
So shall I sing, as time's last moments flee
Now and for ever, Lord, I rest with Thee!

ADOLPH MORAHT

LOOKING TO JESUS.

"HE is brought as a lamb to the slaughter, and as a sheep before her shearers is dumb, so he openeth not his mouth."—ISAIAH 53 : 7.

"O STILLES Lamm."

O SILENT Lamb! for me Thou hast endured,
Jesus, Thou holy, perfect, sinless One!

Thy grief and bitter anguish have secured
My soul's salvation, when this race is run.
Then, let me, to Thine image true,
Thus meekly suffer, with the crown in view.

The narrow way that leads us up to heaven,
Must here through strife and tribulation lie;
Then on the thorny path may strength be given,
This sinful flesh, O Lord, to crucify.
Oh! take this feebleness away,
And make me strong to meet each future day!

Here, daily crosses come to try our weakness,
Here, every member must some burden bear;
But, O my Saviour, if I take with meekness,
The cross appointed by Thy love and care,
Too great, too long, it will not be,
For it is weigh'd and measured out by Thee.

If thus we journey patiently through sadness,
Each grief will make us dearer to our Lord;
But if we flee the cross, in search of gladness,
We can not shun His dread, avenging sword.
Oh! blessed they who hear the call,
Who take the cross, and follow, leaving all!

So help me, Lord, Thy holy will to suffer,
And still a learner at Thy feet to be;
Give faith and patience when the way is rougher,
And at the end a joyful victory.
Thus grief itself is changed to song,
Ofttimes on earth, but evermore ere long.

KARL HEINRICH VON BOGATZKI.

PRAISE.

"LET every thing that hath breath praise the Lord. Praise ye the Lord."—PSALM 150 : 6.

"LOBE den Herren!"

PRAISE to Jehovah! the almighty King of
Creation!
Swell heaven's chorus, chime in every
heart, every nation!
O my soul! wake—
Harp, lute, and psaltery take,
Sound forth in glad adoration.

Praise to Jehovah! whose love o'er thy
course is attending,
Redeeming thy life, and thee from all evil
defending.
Through all the past,
O my soul! over thee cast,
His sheltering wings were bending!

Praise to Jehovah! whose fence has been
planted around thee,
Who, from His heavens, with blessing and
mercy has crowned thee.
Think, happy one!
What He can do, and has done,
Since in His pity He found thee.

Praise to Jehovah! all that has breath praise
Him, sing praises;
Bless God, O my soul, and all that is in me,
sing praises.
In Him rejoice,
Until for ever thy voice
The hymn of eternity raises!

JOACHIM NEANDER.

HYMN SUNG AT A FUNERAL.

"HERE we have no continuing city, but we seek one to come."—HEB. 13 : 14.

"WOHLAUF! wohlan! zum letzten Sang,
Kurz ist der Weg, die Ruhe ist lang."

COME forth! come on, with solemn song!
The road is short, the rest is long!
The Lord brought here, He calls away ·
Make no delay,
This home was for a passing day.

Here in an inn a stranger dwelt,
Here joy and grief by turns he felt;
Poor dwelling, now we close thy door!
The task is o'er,
The sojourner returns no more!

Now of a lasting home possest,
He goes to seek a deeper rest.
Good-night! the day was sultry here,
In toil and fear,
Good-night! the night is cool and clear.

Chime on, ye bells! again begin,
And ring the Sabbath morning in,
The laborer's week-day work is done,
The rest begun,
Which Christ hath for His people won!

Now open to us, gates of peace!
Here let the pilgrim's journey cease.
Ye quiet slumberers, make room
In your still home,
For the new stranger who has come!

How many graves around us lie!
How many homes are in the sky!
Yes, for each saint doth Christ prepare
A place with care:
Thy home is waiting, brother, there!

Jesus, Thou reignest, Lord alone,
Thou wilt return and claim Thine own.
Come quickly, Lord! return again!
Amen! Amen!
Thine seal us ever, now and then!

F. Sachse.

RESURRECTION.

"THIS corruptible must put on incorruption, and this mortal must put on immortality."—1 COR. 15 : 53.

"AUFERSTEHN, ja auferstehn."

THOU shalt rise! my dust, thou shalt arise!
Not always closed thine eyes;
Thy life's first Giver
Will give thee life for ever.
Ah! praise His name!

Sown in darkness, but to bloom again.
When, after winter's reign,
Jesus is reaping
The seed now quietly sleeping.
Ah! praise His name!

Day of praise! for thee, thou wondrous day,
In my quiet grave I stay;
And when I number
My days and nights of slumber,
Thou wakest me!

Then, as they who dream, we shall arise
With Jesus to the skies,
And find that morrow,
The weary pilgrim's sorrow
All past and gone!

Then, with the Holiest I tread,
By my Redeemer led,
    Through Heaven soaring,
    His holy name adoring
        Eternally!

KLOPSTOCK.

HERE AND THERE.

"EYE hath not seen, nor ear heard, neither have entered into the heart of man, the things which God hath prepared for them that love him."—1 COR. 2 : 9.

"WAS kein Auge hat gesehen."

WHAT no human eye hath seen,
  What no mortal ear hath heard,
What on thought hath never been
  In its noblest flights conferred—
This hath God prepared in store
For His people evermore!

When the shaded pilgrim-land
  Fades before my closing eye,
Then reveal'd on either hand
  Heaven's own scenery shall lie
Then the veil of flesh shall fall,
Now concealing, darkening all.

Heavenly landscapes, calmly bright,
  Life's pure river murmuring low,
Forms of loveliness and light,
  Lost to earth long time ago;
Yes, mine own, lamented long,
Shine amid the angel throng!

Many a joyful sight was given,
  Many a lovely vision here—
Hill, and vale, and starry even,
  Friendship's smile, Affection's tear;
These were shadows, sent in love,
Of realities above!

When upon my wearied ear
  Earth's last echoes faintly die,
Then shall angel-harps draw near—
  All the chorus of the sky;
Long-hushed voices blend again,
Sweetly, in that welcome-strain.

Here were sweet and varied tones,
  Bird, and breeze, and fountain's fall,
Yet creation's travail-groans
  Ever sadly sigh'd through all.
There no discord jars the air—
Harmony is perfect there!

When this aching heart shall rest,
  All its busy pulses o'er,

From her mortal robes undrest
  Shall my spirit upward soar.
Then shall unimagined joy
All my thoughts and powers employ.

Here devotion's healing balm
  Often came to soothe my breast—
Hours of deep and holy calm,
  Earnests of eternal rest.
But the bliss was here unknown,
Which shall there be all my own!

Jesus reigns, the Life, the Sun
  Of that wondrous world above;
All the clouds and storms are gone,
  All is light, and all is love.
All the shadows melt away
In the blaze of perfect day! LANGE.

JOY IN BELIEVING.

"If any man be in Christ, he is a new creature." — 1 Cor. 5:17.

"Ich glaube, Hallelujah!"

Hallelujah! I believe!
  Now the giddy world stands fast,
Now my soul has found an anchor
  Till the night of storm is past.
All the gloomy mists are rising,
  And a clue is in my hand,
Through earth's labyrinth to guide me
  To a bright and heavenly land.

Hallelujah! I believe!
  Sorrow's bitterness is o'er,
And affliction's heavy burden
  Weighs my spirit down no more.
On the cross the mystic writing
  Now revealed before me lies,
And I read the words of comfort,
  "As a father, I chastise."

Hallelujah! I believe!
  Now no longer on my soul
All the debt of sin is lying—
  One great Friend has paid the whole!

Ice-bound fields of legal labor
  I have left, with all their toil;
While the fruits of love are growing
  From a new and genial soil.

Hallelujah! I believe!
  Now life's mystery is gone,
Gladly through its fleeting shadows,
  To the end I journey on.
Through the tempest or the sunshine,
  Over flowers or ruins led,
Still the path is *homeward* hasting,
  Where all sorrow shall have fled.

Hallelujah! I believe!
  Now, O Love! I know thy power,
Thine no false or fragile fetters,
  Not the rose-wreaths of an hour!
Christian bonds of holy union,
  Death itself does not destroy;
Yes, to live, and love forever,
  Is our heritage of joy!

MÖWES.

LOWLY.

"Blessed are the poor in spirit: for theirs is the kingdom of heaven."—Matt. 5: 3.

"Hinab geht Christi Weg."

Christ's path was sad and lowly,
But yet thou, in thy pride,
Wouldst climb the highest summit,
And on the hight abide!
Wouldst thou to heaven arise?
Thy Lord the way will show thee;
For who would climb these skies,
Must first with Him be lowly.

Lowly, my soul, be lowly—
Follow the paths of old:
The feather riseth lightly,
But never so the gold!
The stream, descending fast,
Has gathered, quietly, slowly—
A river rolls at last—
Therefore, my soul, be lowly.

Lowly, my eyes, be lowly:
God, from His throne above,
Looks down upon the humble,
In kindness and in love.

Still, as I rise, I shall
  Have greater depths below me,
And haughty looks must fall—
  Therefore, mine eyes, be lowly.

Lowly, my hands, be lowly:
  Christ's poor around us dwell,
Stoop down, and kindly cherish
  The flock He loves so well.
Not toiling to secure
  This world's fame and glory—
Thy Saviour blessed the poor,
  Therefore, my hands, be lowly.

Lowly, my heart, be lowly:
  So God shall dwell with thee;
It is the meek and patient
  Who shall exalted be.
Deep in the valley rest
  The Spirit's gifts most holy,
And they who seek are blest—
  Therefore, my heart, be lowly

Lowly, I would be lowly!
  This frame, to earth allied,
Must first to dust be humbled
  Ere it be glorified!
My God, prepare me here
  For all that lies before me;
I would in heaven appear,
  And so I would be lowly.

INGOLSTELLER.

THE CHRISTIAN CROSS.

"Then said Jesus unto his disciples, If any man will come after me, let him deny himself, and take up his cross, and follow me."—Matt. 16:24.

"Der Christen Schmuck und Ordensband."

The Christian's badge of honor here,
Has ever been the cross;
And when its hidden joys appear,
He counts it gain, not loss.

He bears it meekly, as is best,
While struggling here with sin;
He wears it not upon his breast,
Ah! no, it is within.

And if it bring him pain or shame,
He takes it joyfully,
For well he knows from whom it came
And what its end shall be.

Only a little while 'tis borne,
And as a a pledge is given,
Of robes of triumph, to be worn
For evermore in heaven.

Spitta.

SONG OF THE SOJOURNER.

"I AM a stranger with thee and a sojourner, as all my fathers were."—PSALM 39:12.

"Ich bin ein Gast auf Erden."

A PILGRIM and a stranger,
I journey here below;
Far distant is my country,
The home to which I go.
Here I must toil and travel,
Oft weary and opprest,
But there my God shall lead me
To everlasting rest.

I've met with storms and danger,
Even from my early years,
With enemies and conflicts,
With fightings and with fears.
There's nothing here that tempts me
To wish a longer stay,
So I must hasten forwards,
No halting or delay.

It is a well-worn pathway—
Many have gone before:
The holy saints and prophets,
The patriarchs of yore.

They trod the toilsome journey
  In patience and in faith;
And them I fain would follow,
  Like them in life and death!

Who would share Abraham's blessing,
  Must Abraham's path pursue,
A stranger and a pilgrim,
  Like him, must journey through.
The foes must be encountered,
  The dangers must be passed;
Only a faithful soldier
  Receives the crown at last.

So I must hasten forwards—
  Thank God, the end will come!
This land of my sojourning
  Is not my destined home.
That ever more abideth,
  Jerusalem above,
The everlasting city,
  The land of light and love.

There still my thoughts are dwelling,
  'Tis there I long to be!
Come, Lord, and call Thy servant
  To blessedness with Thee!
Come, bid my toils be ended,
  Let all my wanderings cease;
Call from the wayside lodging,
  To the sweet home of peace!

There I shall dwell forever,
No more a stranger guest,
With all Thy blood-bought children
In everlasting rest.
The pilgrim toils forgotten,
The pilgrim conflicts o'er,
All earthly griefs behind us,
Eternal joys before!

PAUL GERHARDT.

THE CHRISTIAN HOUSEHOLD

"And they constrained Him, saying, Abide with us."—LUKE 24 : 29.

"O SELIG Haus, wo man dich aufgenommen."

O HAPPY house! where Thou art loved the best,
Dear Friend and Saviour of our race,
Where never comes such welcomed honored Guest,
Where none can ever fill Thy place;
Where every heart goes forth to meet Thee,
Where every ear attends Thy word,
Where every lip with blessing greets Thee,
Where all are waiting on their Lord.

O happy house! where two are one in
heart,
In faith and hope are one,
Whom death can only for a little part,
Not end the union here begun;
Who share together one salvation,
Who would be with Thee, Lord, always,
In gladness or in tribulation,
In happy or in evil days.

O happy house! whose little ones are given
Early to Thee, in faith and prayer—
To Thee, their Friend, who from the hights
of heaven
Guards them with more than mother's
care.
O happy house! where little voices
Their glad hosannas love to raise,
And childhood's lisping tongue rejoices
To bring new songs of love and praise.

O happy house! and happy servitude!
Where all alike one Master own;
Where daily duty, in Thy strength pursued,
Is never hard nor toilsome known;
Where each one serves Thee, meek and
lowly,
Whatever Thine appointment be,
Till common tasks seem great and holy,
When they are done as unto Thee.

O happy house! where Thou art not forgot
 When joy is flowing full and free;
O happy house! where every wound is
  brought,
 Physician, Comforter, to Thee.
Until at last, earth's day's-work ended,
 All meet Thee in that home above,
From whence Thou camest, where Thou
  hast ascended,
 Thy heaven of glory and of love!

SPITTA.

THE TWO JOURNEYS.

"THEN shall ye return, and discern between the righteous and the wicked; between him that serveth God, and him that serveth him not."—MAL. 3 : 18.

"WOHIN, wohin?"

"WHITHER, oh! whither?" "With blind-
  folded eyes,
 Down a wild torrent under stormy skies,
 A gulf between two dark eternities,
  Drifting, we know not where!"

"Whither oh! whither?" "To a land of
  light,
 A home of loveliness serene and bright,
 Joyfully hastening with steady flight,
  Our hearts before us there!"

"Whither, oh! whither?" "Life's short pleasures past,
Hope's funeral knell the sound on every blast,
Heaven's entrance closed, to ruin hurried fast,
A leaf before the wind!"

"Whither, oh! whither?" "Pilgrims near their home,
No longer in a foreign land to roam;
Bright and beloved ones waiting till we come,
All sorrow left behind!"

"Whither, oh! whither?" "Who the path can say
To where some star will lend a cheering ray?
Or through earth's labyrinth direct our way,
So wildly sought in vain!"

"Whither, oh! whither?" "Christ the risen One,
Through life and death, hath now to glory gone,
He sends His messengers to lead us on—
The way is broad and plain!"

"Whither, oh! whither?" "Terrible reply
From yon white throne of judgment in
the sky:
'Depart, accursed! from my presence fly
Forever'—awful word!"

"Whither, oh! whither?" Washed from
earthly stain,
No more to wander or to fall again;
Forever with the Father to remain,
Forever with the Lord!"

MÖWES.

A LITTLE WHILE.

"A LITTLE while, and ye shall not see me: and again a little while, and ye shall see me; because I go to the Father."
—JOHN 16:16.

"UEBER ein kleines!" so sprach Er in naechtlicher Stunde.

"A LITTLE while!"—so spake our gracious
Lord
To the sad band around that sacred
board,
While His long-burdened heart
Already felt the smart
Of His own Father's sin-avenging sword.

'Tis for thee also, weeping, weary one!
Are not all things around thee hastening on?
Thy Father's hand ordains
All these, thy griefs and pains —
"A little while!"—they, too, are past and gone.

Have all the lights of love quite died away?
Has thy last star withdrawn its cheering ray?
Till the long night wears past,
Weeping and prayer must last;
But joy approaches with the dawning day.

Do friends misunderstand, or mock thy pain?
Hast thou too fondly trusted, loved in vain?
The Faithful One and True
Can blighted hopes renew,
And hearts long severed reünite again.

"A little while!"—the fetters clasp no more,
The spirit, long enthralled, is free to soar,
And takes its joyful flight,
On radiant wings of light,
To the blest mansions of the heavenly shore.

There end the longings of the weary
breast,
The good sought after here is there
possest;
Ride o'er the stormy sea,
Poor bark! soon shalt thou be
In the calm haven of eternal rest.

"A little while!" look forward and hope
on!
Soon shall the troubled dreams of night
be gone.
The shadows pass away
Before the abiding day,
The Saviour comes, to claim and bless
His own! META HÄUSER.

SHADOW AND SUBSTANCE.

"BUT the word of the Lord endureth forever. And this is the word which by the Gospel is preached unto you."—1 PET. 1:25.

"DAS Leben ist gleich einem Traum."

THIS life is like a flying dream,
Or like the vapor from the stream,
Or like the grass that grows to-day,
But fades away,
When winds across it roughly play.

Only Thyself, my God, art now
Just as Thou wert—my Refuge Thou—
Though rock and mountain be destroyed,
There is no void,
With Thy loved presence still enjoyed.

Thus sojourning in this low scene,
Upon my Saviour I would lean,
And learn as moments quickly fly,
Self to deny,
Dead to the world, before I die.

Vain joys, away! yea, spread your wings
For I have tasted better things.
I seek a portion all divine,
Ever to shine;
Lord Jesus make me wholly Thine.

JOACHIM NEANDER.

THE MISSIONARY ON THE SEA SHORE.

"AND a vision appeared to Paul in the night: There stood a man of Macedonia, and prayed him, saying, Come over into Macedonia, and help us."—ACTS 16 : 9.

"WIE schaumt so feierlich zu unsern Fuessen."

DARK mighty Ocean, rolling to our feet!
In thy low murmur many voices meet,
The sound of distant lands brought strange-
ly near
To Fancy's ear.

From shores unknown comes the sweet
Sabbath bell,
New languages the old glad tidings tell,
We hear the hymn of praise—the martyr's
song—
All borne along.

And starting at the summons, we obey,
And o'er thy waves prepare to find our way,
Leaving the ties of country and of home,
Ocean, we come!

Our chariot thou, to bear us to the lands
Where fields of promise wait our willing
hands;
Thou and ourselves are servants, to fulfill
Our Master's will!

And whether in thy depths we find a grave,
Or with our heart's-blood dye the distant
wave,
Or with glad hopes, upon thy billows borne,
Homewards return;

Whether to death or life our course leads
on—
The Master knows—His holy will be done!
To life eternal, when all storms are past,
We come at last!

F. DE LA MOTTE FOUQUÉ.

SABBATH MORNING HYMN.

"THIS is the day which the Lord hath made; we will rejoice and be glad in it."—PSALM 118:24.

"HALLELUJAH! Schoener Morgen!"

HALLELUJAH! Fairest morning,
Fairer than my words can say,
Down I lay the heavy burden
Of life's toil and care to-day;
While this morn of joy and love
Brings fresh vigor from above.

Sunday, full of holy glory!
  Sweetest rest-day of the soul,
Light upon a darkened world
  From thy blessed moments roll.
Holy, happy heavenly day,
Thou canst charm my grief away!

Now I taste my Father's goodness,
  Falling like the morning dew,
While of pastures even fairer
  I would take a distant view;
Where my Shepherd's flock I see,
Where my dwelling soon shall be!

Oh! be silent, earthly turmoil,
  I have work more sweet and blest,
And each thought would gather homeward
  On this happy day of rest.
Thus with clearer faith to see
All my Lord has done for me.

In the gladness of His worship,
  I will seek my joy to-day:
It is then I learn the fullness
  Of the grace for which I pray;
When the word of life is given
Like the Saviour's voice from heaven.

Let the day's sweet hours be ended
  Prayerfully, as they began;
And Thy blessing, Lord, be granted,
  Till earth's days and weeks are done;
That at last Thy servant may
Keep eternal Sabbath day.

SCHMOLK.

CHARITY.

"AND the King shall answer and say unto them, Verily I say unto you, Inasmuch as ye have done it unto one of the least of these my brethren, ye have done it unto me."—MATT. 25:40.

"CHRIST! wenn die Armen manchesmal."

AH Christian! if the needy poor
  Have e'er unheeded been,
Beware lest at thy closed door
  The Saviour stood unseen.

Let heart and house be open thrown,
  Thy gifts with others share;
Let holy charity be shown
  To all who need thy care.

Then, while thy glance abroad is cast,
  The Lord is by thy side;
For through the open door He passed
  Because it was so wide.

And ere thy beating heart can guess
Who entered by the door,
His gracious hands are raised to bless
Thy basket and thy store;

To bless thee all time's little day,
With His almighty love:
To bless the long eternity
That waits for thee above—

Where soon the pearly gates, which stand,
To all He'll open throw,
Who, for His sake, with willing hand,
Did minister below.

HEY.

WE TOO ARE THINE.

"THE Lord reigneth; let the earth rejoice."—PSALM 97:1.

"HERR, unser Gott, mit Ehrfurcht dienen."

LORD our God, in reverence lowly,
The hosts of heaven call Thee "holy."
From cherubim and seraphim,
From angel phalanx, far extending,
In fuller tones is still ascending
The "holy, holy," of their hymn.

The fount of joy Thou art,
Ever filling every heart,
Ever! ever!
We too are Thine, and with them sing,
"Thou, Lord, and only Thou art King."

Lord, there are bending now before Thee
The elders, with their crowned glory,
The first-born of the blessed band.
There, too, earth's ransomed and forgiven
Brought by the Saviour safe to heaven,
In glad unnumbered myriads stand.
Loud are the songs of praise
Their mingled voices raise,
Ever! ever!
We too are Thine, and with them sing,
"Thou, Lord, and only Thou art King."

They sing in sweet, and sinless numbers,
The wondrous love that never slumbers,
And of the wisdom, power, and might,
The truth and faithfulness abiding,
And over all Thy works presiding.
But they can scarcely praise aright;
For all is never sung,
Even by seraph's tongue,
Never! never!
We too are Thine, and with them sing,
"Thou, Lord, and only Thou art King."

Oh! come, reveal Thyself more fully,
That we may learn to praise more truly;
Make every heart a temple true,
Filled with Thy glory overflowing,
More of Thy love each morning showing,
And waking praises loud and new—
Here let Thy peace divine
Over Thy children shine,
Ever! ever!
And glad or sad, we joining sing,
"Thou, Lord, and only Thou art King."

G. TERSTEEGEN.

SUBMISSION.

"IT is the Lord; let him do what seemeth him good."—SAM. 3:18.

"Du sollst," so sprach der Herr, "du sollst ermatten."

THUS said the Lord: "Thy days of health are over!"
And, like the mist, my vigor fled away;
Till but a feeble shadow was remaining,
A fragile form, fast hasting to decay.
The May of life, with all its blooming flowers—
The joys of life, in colors bright arrayed—
The hopes of life, in all their airy promise—

I saw them in the distance slowly fade:
Then sighs of sorrow in my soul would rise,
Then silent tears would overflow my eyes!
But a warm sunbeam, from a higher sphere,
Stole through the gloom, and dried up every tear.
Is this Thy will, good Lord?—the strife is o'er,
Thy servant weeps no more.

"Thy cherished flock thou mayest feed no longer!"—
Thus said the Lord, who gave them to my hand;
Nor even was my sinking heart permitted
To ask the reason of the stern command.
The Shepherd's rod had been so gladly carried,
The flock had followed long, and loved it well:
Alas! the hour was dark, the stroke was heavy,
When sudden from my nerveless grasp it fell.
Then sighs of sorrow in my soul would rise,
Then rushing tears would overflow my eyes!

But I beheld *Thee*, O my Lord and God!
Beneath the Cross, lay down the Shepherd's rod;
Is this Thy will, good Lord?—the strife is o'er,
Thy servant weeps no more.

"*Never again* thou mayest feed my people!"
Thus said the Lord, with countenance severe;
And bade me lay aside, at once, forever,
The robes of office, honored long and dear.
The sacred mantle from my shoulders falling,
The sacred girdle loosening at His word,
I could but think and say, while sadly gazing,
I *have been* once a pastor of the Lord!
Then groans of anguish in my soul would rise,
Then burning tears would overflow my eyes!
But His own garment once was torn away,
To the rude soldiery a spoil and prey;
Is this Thy will, good Lord?—the strife is o'er,
Thy servant weeps no more.

"From the calm port of safety rudely severed,
Through stormy waves thy shattered bark must go,
And dimly see, amid the darkness sinking,
Nothing but heaven above, and depths below!"
Thus said the Lord — and through a raging ocean
Of doubts and fears my spirit toiled in vain.
Ah! many a dove went forth, of hope inquiring.
But none with olive leaf returned again!
Then groans of anguish in my soul would rise,
Then tears of bitterness o'erflowed my eyes!
But through the gloom the promised light was given,
From the dark waves I *could* look up to heaven:
Is this Thy will, good Lord?—the strife is o'er,
Thy servant weeps no more.

"Thou shalt find kindred hearts, in love united,
And with them in the wilderness rejoice.

Yet stand prepared, each gentle tie untwining,
To separate, at my commanding voice."
Thus said the Lord—He gave, as He had promised—
How many a loving heart has met my own!
But, ever must the tender bonds be broken,
And each go forwards, distant and alone!
Then sighs of sorrow in my soul would rise,
Then tears of anguish overflowed my eyes!—
But Thou hast known the bitter parting day,
From the beloved John hast turned away—
Is this Thy will, good Lord?—the strife is o'er,
Thy servant weeps no more.

MÖWES.

These stanzas were written by the devoted pastor, Heinrich Moewes, in 1832, when obliged by illness to resign the ministerial office.

A PASTOR'S PARTING WORDS.

"To me to live is Christ, and to die is gain."—PHIL. 1:21.

"MERKT Ihr's, Freunde! Mein Auge wird muede."

HEAR me, my friends! the hour has come,
Soon I must leave you, and hasten home;
Then, ere our Father shall call me to rest,
Hear my last wishes, my last request.

When my last moments on earth draw near,
When my own voice you no longer hear,
Then gather round me, and sing the song
We have sung together and loved so long.

Sing of His love, who has died to save,
Him who has entered and spoiled the grave;
Sing with glad accents and grateful heart,
Sing till my spirit in peace depart.

Fold my cold hands on my quiet breast,
Close my tired eyelids in gentle rest,
One farewell kiss of affection take—
Leave me to slumber till Christ shall awake.

To our last dwelling-place bear me along
With sweetest music of chimes and song;
There let the evergreen branches wave,
And bright flowers blossom around my
grave.

Though a long darkness has veiled my
eyes,
Still let them look to the eastern skies;
There, where the Morning Star rose
bright,
Jesus, the Sun of our darkest night.

Carve but these words on the simple
stone,
"*Living and dying, of Jesus alone*
Ever he spoke to the Church beneath;
Sweet to him, therefore, was life and
death."

When ye revisit the peaceful spot,
Come with soft tears and with tender
thought;
Look up to heaven in hope and prayer—
Jesus again will unite us there!

MÖWES.

BE THOU MY FRIEND.

"Henceforth, I call you not servants, but I have called you friends."—John 15 : 15.

"Sey du mein Freund, und schau in meine Brust.'

Be Thou my Friend, and look upon my
heart,
Lord Jesus, Son of man!
Each seed of good or ill that there has part
Do Thou in mercy scan.
The burning springs there lurking,
O Lord! Thou canst control,
And each wild passion, working
Within my sinful soul.

In mortal weakness, once was veiled Thy
might,
Light of Eternal Day!
Before Thee lay temptation's dreary fight,
And yet, Thou wentst that way!
And Thou couldst weep with sorrow,
Or share our bridal mirth,
And yet no tarnish borrow
From this polluted earth.

Beneath Thy feet the realms of earth were
spread,
All bathed in golden gloss;

One word had laid their crowns upon Thy
 head,
 Yet, Thou couldst choose the cross!
 And from Thy throne descending,
 Couldst take the pilgrim's path,
 And with Thy hosts attending,
 Couldst die a murderer's death!

How the world hated Thee, and vengeance
 hurled
 Against Thee, great Unknown!
How Thou didst love this poor and blinded
 world,
 And bought her for Thine own!
 Her arrows pierced through Thee,
 From cruel, willing hands;
 Yet Thou wouldst draw her to Thee
 With loving, gentle bands.

Thou hast returned, all pure and holy,
 home,
 My Brother, and my Lord!
And when with trembling to Thy throne I
 come,
 My Refuge is Thy word.
 There, by Thine arm fast holding,
 And hidden, by Thy grace,
 Within Thy robes deep folding,
 Let me behold God's face.

Yes! be my Friend, and look upon my heart,
On all that's hidden there;
The deeper guilt that stings me with its dart,
The unknown sins I bear,
The passions that distress me,
Let Thy pure presence slay;
The sorrows that oppress me
Before Thee flee away.

Oh! shine upon me with Thy holy light,
When gathering gloom I see,
And leave me not in tribulation's night,
But send sweet peace to me!
The chains of sin dissever,
Blind fancy's wildest play;
Then, then, my Lord, forever
Take grief and sin away! LANGE.

AS THOU WILT.

"THE will of the Lord be done."—ACTS 21:14.

"WIE Gott will! also will ich sagen."

As Thou wilt, my God! I ever say;
What Thou wilt is ever best for me;
What have I to do with earthly care,
Since to-morrow I may leave with Thee?
Lord, Thou knowest, I am not my own,
All my hope and help depend on Thee alone.

As Thou wilt! still I can believe;
Never did the word of promise fail.
Faith can hold it fast, and feel it sure,
Though temptations cloud and fears assail.
Why art thou disquieted, O my soul?
When thy Father knows, and rules the whole.

As Thou wilt! still I can endure;
Patiently my daily cross can bear;
Why should I complain, a pardoned child,
If the children's portion here I share?
As Thou wilt, my Father and my God!
I can drink the cup, and kiss the rod.

As Thou wilt! still I can hope on.
Sunshine may return when storms have past;
Thine All-seeing Eye of sleepless love
Watches o'er my path from first to last
When Thou wilt, upon the desert plain
Springs may rise anew, and rivers flow again.

As Thou wilt! all life's journey through,
To Thy will my own I would resign;
If on earth I have but little store,
Be it so! all heaven shall be mine;
Or if but Thyself, my God, art given,
Nothing more I need, or ask in earth or heaven.

As Thou wilt! when Thine hour has come,
Let Thy servant, Lord, in peace depart;
Good it is to love and serve Thee here,
Better to be with Thee where Thou art.
When, or where, or how the call may be,
It will not come too early or too late for me.

As Thou wilt, O Lord! I ask no more.
With the promise, Faith pursues her way;
Patience can endure through sorrow's night,
Hope can look beyond to heaven's own day,
Love can wait, and trust, and labor still;
Life and death shall be, according to Thy will!

NEUMEISTER.

SABBATH HYMN.

"I was in the Spirit on the Lord's day."—Rev. 1:10.

"Zeige Dich uns ohne Huelle."

LORD, remove the veil away,
Let us see Thyself to-day!
Thou who camest from on high,
For our sins to bleed and die,
Help us now to cast aside
All that would our hearts divide,
With the Father and the Son
Let Thy living Church be one.

Oh! from earthly cares set free,
Let us find our rest in Thee!
May our cares and conflicts cease
In the calm of Sabbath peace,
That Thy people, here below,
Something of the bliss may know,
Something of the rest and love
In the Sabbath-home above.

From beyond the grave's dark night
What mild radiance meets my sight?
Softly stealing on the ear,
What strange music do I hear!
'Tis the golden crowns on high,
'Tis the chorus of the sky!
Lord, Thy sinful child prepare
For a place and portion there.

Give my soul the spotless dress
Of Thy perfect righteousness;
Then at length, a welcome guest,
I shall enter to the feast,
Take the harp and raise the song,
All Thy ransomed ones among;
Earthly cares and sorrows o'er,
Joys to last for evermore!

KLOPSTOCK

WHAT PLEASES GOD.

"Whatsoever the Lord pleased, that did he in heaven, and in earth, in the seas, and all deep places."—Psalm 135 : 6.

"Was Gott gefaellt, mein frommes Kind."

What God decrees, child of His love,
Take patiently, though it may prove
The storm that wrecks thy treasure here,
Be comforted! thou needst not fear
What pleases God.

The wisest will is God's own will;
Rest on this anchor, and be still;
For peace around thy path shall flow,
When only wishing here below
What pleases God.

The truest heart is God's own heart,
Which bids thy grief and fear depart;
Protecting, guiding, day and night,
The soul that welcomes here aright
What pleases God.

Oh! could I sing, as I desire,
My grateful voice should never tire,
To tell the wondrous love and power,
Thus working out, from hour to hour,
What pleases God.

The King of kings, He rules on earth,
He sends us sorrow here, or mirth,
He bears the ocean in His hand;
And thus we meet, on sea or land,
What pleases God.

His Church on earth He dearly loves,
Although He oft its sin reproves;
The rod itself, His love can speak,
He smites till we return to seek
What pleases God.

Then let the crowd around thee seize
The joys that for a season please,
But willingly their paths forsake,
And for thy blessed portion take
What pleases God.

Art thou despised by all around?
Do tribulations here abound?
Jesus will give the victory,
Because His eye can see in thee
What pleases God.

Thy heritage is safe in heaven:
There, shall the crown of joy be given;
There, shalt thou hear, and see, and know,
As thou couldst never here below,
What pleases God.

GERHARDT.

AT LAST.

"For surely there is an end; and thine expectation shall not be cut off."—Prov. 23 : 18.

"Zuletzt geht's wohl."

At last all shall be well with those, His own,
  Whom Christ from sin and Satan has made free;
  At last shall come the year of jubilee,
The time of rest, when all their fears are flown.

At last shall come the glory and reward,
  When we have stood the world's reproach and loss,
  When faith and love have meekly borne the cross,
And the good servants are made like their Lord.

At last the soldier shall receive his crown,
  Brought from the field, home to his fatherland;
  Forever in a peaceful lot to stand,
His foes all vanquished, and his arms laid down.

At last the water shall be turned to wine,
And all the marriage guests, in bliss above,
The wonders trace of God's redeeming love,
His counsels all fulfilled, and plans divine.

At last, not yet, into the heavenly rest
The Lord shall lead His saints, and give them there,
Made like the angels, angel joys to share,
Ever with Him and with each other blest.

At last, not yet;—O weary heart, be still!
Trust to thy God, thy Saviour, and thy Friend,
Who chastens now, but loves unto the end.
So be it, Lord! good is Thy holy will.

C. A. BERNSTEIN.

THE GRAVEYARD.

"WEEP ye not for the dead, neither bemoan him."—JER. 22 : 10.

"ICH weiss ein stilles, liebes Land."

I KNOW a sweet and silent spot,
  And gladly there I stay,
Though many near me heed it not,
  Or wish it far away.

'Tis but a narrow strip of land,
  Hedged in, and decked with flowers;
Yet all round it tokens stand,
  Of other world than ours.

These little mounds men scarcely see,
  Nor dream of gold concealed;
But they are precious mines to me,
  Where treasures vast are sealed.

Here, as beside some boundary-stone,
  The child of troubled time
Looks upward, where his friends are gone,
  And seeks their brighter clime.

Here, I have gathered strength and light
  For all my future way;
Here, faith is nearly turned to sight,
  And night almost to day.

And not afar, I see the day
  Which daily draws more near,
When passing friends shall pause, and say,
  "Our brother's grave is here!"

But I'll have journeyed, glad and free,
  Far from this silent spot,
While leaving to its sanctuary
  What other's hands have brought;

And in my Father's happy land
  Have met my own once more,
Where we shall scarcely understand
  Why we have wept before.

LANGE.

FUNERAL HYMN.

"Then shall the dust return to the earth as it was; and the spirit shall return to God who gave it."—Eccles. 12:

"Lebwohl! die Erde wartet dein."

Beloved and honored, fare thee well!
Go in thy last long home to dwell;
Softly our loving hands prepare
Thy narrow bed—sleep softly there!

Love looks below, with weeping eyes,
Where her long-cherished treasure lies.
Our sweet companionship is o'er,
Our pilgrim friend returns no more!

Earth takes her own—this mortal frame;
Eternity her part shall claim;
And so we say, in humble trust,
The soul to God—the dust to dust.

Then, looking up through sorrow's night,
We trace the spirit's homeward flight;
The Prince of Life has marked that road,
Through the dark valley, home to God.

Where once the Master lowly lay,
Let the tired servant rest to-day,
And in the Father's house above
Forever share his Master's love.

Thanks for thy joy, all danger past!
Thanks for our own good hope at last!
Weeping endureth for a night,
Joy cometh with the morning light.

Lord, will that morning soon appear?
May our own summons now be near?
Shall sorrow soon be past and gone?
Thy will be done! Thy will be done!

Only prepare us, all Thy will
Gladly to suffer, or fulfill;
Then call us to Thy heavenly rest,
With thee, and with our brother blest.

F. SACHSE.

MINISTERING ANGELS.

"ARE they not all ministering spirits, sent forth to minister for them who shall be heirs of salvation?"—HEB. 1 : 14.

"UM die Erd' und um ihr Kinder."

ROUND this earth, and round her children,
  Floats a spirit land unseen;
When our earthly course is ended,
  When the veil shall rise between,
When we cross this mortal threshold,
  When we take our heavenward way,
Angel brothers shall uphold us—
  Brothers of Eternity.

God's own children, pure and holy!
  You the messengers He sends;
'Tis an ever sweet remembrance,
  That you are our guardian friends,—
That you watch our life-long journey,
  That, unseen, you oft are near,
Holy thoughts and deeds to strengthen,
  Or to dry the mourner's tear.

Who would not retreat in terror
  From the evil yet undone;
Who not turn with shame and mourning,
  From the evil course begun?
Who would e'er be found forgetful
  Of his calling and his vow,
If the thought had only risen,
  "Angels are among us now?"

Rise, my soul, in heart to meet them,
  When this earth would chain thee fast;
Rise among these free-born spirits,
  When her coils are round thee cast.
Be courageous, 'tis thy journey
  Out of darkness into light;
God and angels are around thee,
  Tremble not, but rise and fight.

SPERL.

THE MIDNIGHT CRY.

"And what I say unto you, I say unto all, Watch."—Mark 13 : 37.

"Der Herr bricht ein, um Mitternacht."

The Lord shall come in dead of night,
  When all is stillness round;
How happy they whose lamps are bright,
  Who hail the trumpet's sound!

How blind and dead the world appears!
  How deep her slumbers are!
Still dreaming that the day she fears
  Is distant and afar!

Who spends his day in holy toil?
  His talent used aright,
That he may haste, with heavenly spoi.
  To meet his Lord that night?

Are ye arousing from their sleep,
  The saints who dare to rest,
And calling every one to keep
  A watch more true and blest?

Wake up, my heart and soul, anew,
  Let sleep no moment claim;
But hourly watch, as if ye knew
  This night the Master came.

The Lord shall come in dead of night,
  When all is stillness round;
How happy they whose lamps are bright,
  Who hail the trumpet's sound!
ZINZENDORF.

FOREVER WITH THE LORD.

"AND so shall we ever be with the Lord." -1 THESS. 4:17.

" WIR werden bei dem Herrn seyn allezeit."

O SWEET home-echo on the pilgrim's way,
  Thrice welcome message from a land of
    light!
As through a clouded sky the moonbeams
    stray,
  So on Eternity's deep shrouded night
Streams a mild radiance, from that cheer-
    ing word,
  'So shall we be forever with the Lord."

At home with Jesus! He who went before,
For His own people mansions to prepare;
The soul's deep longings stilled, its conflicts o'er,
All rest and blessedness with Jesus there.
What home like this can the wide earth afford?
"So shall we be forever with the Lord."

With Him all gathered! to that blessed home,
Through all its windings, still the pathway tends;
While ever and anon bright glimpses come
Of that fair city where the journey ends.
Where all of bliss is centred in one word,
"So shall we be forever with the Lord."

Here, kindred hearts are severed far and wide,
By many a weary mile of land and sea,
Or life's all-varied cares, and paths divide;
But yet a joyful gathering shall be,
The broken links repaired, the lost restored,
"So shall we be forever with the Lord."

And is there *ever* perfect union here?
Ah! daily sins, lamented and confest,

They come between us and the friends
most dear,
They mar our blessedness and break our
rest.
With life we leave the evils long deplored:
"So shall we be forever with the Lord."

All prone to error—none set wholly free
From the old serpent's soul-ensnaring
chain,
The truths one child of God can clearly
see,
He seeks to make his brother feel in
vain;
But all shall harmonize in heaven's full
chord,
"So shall we be forever with the Lord."

O blessed promise! mercifully given,
Well may it hush the wail of earthly
woe;
O'er the dark passage to the gates of
heaven
The light of hope and resurrection
throw!
Thanks for the blessed, life-inspiring word,
"So shall we be forever with the Lord."

META HÄUSER.

www.ingramcontent.com/pod-product-compliance
Lightning Source LLC
LaVergne TN
LVHW021403110826
845150LV00007B/1763
* 9 7 8 1 4 2 5 5 1 2 5 8 3 *